MW01593779

Jesus, YOU MAKE THE DARKNESS tremble

Rolena,

Thanks for entering!
God loves you today
and will work
all your needs out!
Trust Him!

Love You!
Beth

2018

Jesus, YOU MAKE THE DARKNESS tremble

Copyright © 2018 by Beth jane
All rights Reserved
Printed in the United States of America

The book is protected under copyright and needs
written permission from the author before any
information is copied-unless for small quotes.

Scripture taken from the New King James
Version®. Copyright © 1982 by Thomas Nelson.
Used by permission. All rights reserved.
"Scripture quotations taken from the
Amplified® Bible (AMP),
Copyright © 2015 by The Lockman Foundation
Used by permission. www.Lockman.org"
Other scriptures taken from the King James
Version-capitalized pronouns linking to God
added by author.

Cover designed by Beth jane. Photos by
@reyas_photography

ISBN 13: 978-1721941575

Note to parents!

I wrote this for all generations, but not all content may be suitable for children. I recommend reading through the book, and then reading over the parts your children can read with them!
Thank you!

All the Glory to God

Table of Contents:

Introduction

Chapter One: One **Solution** for all problems

Chapter Two: The Holy Ghost

Chapter Three: A personal relationship with Jesus

Chapter Four: Forsaking worldly standards

Chapter Five: Some sowing and reaping

Chapter Six: R.E.S.P.E.C.T.

Chapter Seven: Mind Torment, Anxiety, and Depression

Chapter Eight: Judging

Chapter Nine: Relationships

Chapter Ten: Body Image

Chapter Eleven: Love vs Hate

Chapter Twelve: Social Media

Chapter Thirteen: God's calling for YOU

Chapter Fourteen: Jesus is a Healer

Chapter Fifteen: Betrayal

Chapter Sixteen: Rush

Chapter Seventeen: Accepting Jesus' Sacrifice

Chapter Eighteen: Apathy

Chapter Nineteen: Watch and Pray

A word from Beth

*Also I heard the voice of the Lord,
saying:*

*"Whom shall I send,
And who will go for Us?"*

Then I said, "Here am I! Send me."

Isaiah 6:8

Introduction:

Ever felt cornered? Ever felt like no matter how much you ran or how much you tried, you couldn't outrun the darkness?

Have you ever even felt darkness? Felt its sickening hands grip your stomach? Ever felt so down to hear about another school shooting only one week after the last one?

I know a lot of us have felt this. And there is a sad truth about this world…it's dark. It's very dark. And the times we live in are the darkest.

Hurricanes right and left. People can't even get over the first one before another comes.

School shootings…schools have to have shooting drills now.

Evil politicians trying to destroy our countries.

Suicide.

Abuse.

Racial issues.

Human Trafficking.

All in all: it's so very dark.

This is the work of an evil enemy against our souls, the devil. And he knows his time is limited. So he's working hard to destroy us all.

But there is Hope.

Hey, my name is Beth jane and I've been praying for you for a long time.

Let me take you back to about a year ago when I was down at our family pond. There was a long drought where we live, and the water line was way back from where it should be. Much like the state of things around us, *much like our spiritual lives.*

At this time many hurricanes and such were going on. It was a dark time-it still is.

But God led me to start praying what I call the "Wholeheartedly Abandoned" prayer. It started as just being a prayer for my generation, but it grew into more. It grew into a prayer for *all* generations.

I prayed we all would forsake apathy and live wholeheartedly for Jesus. I prayed we all were filled with the Holy Spirit, ect.

Then after praying for many weeks; it rained. And it rained more times weeks after that.

Then we had a real good rain, and…the water came back up.

That's the way our spiritual lives should be. The water needs to come back up. We need to stop letting the water line be low. Be dry. We need to realize that God is what we need and we need to live in Him and *for* Him. Because that's really the best and most special way to ever live.

You see, where there is darkness, there is a Light that is much brighter and much stronger than any force of the enemy.

WE DO NOT HAVE TO DROWN IN DARKNESS. Do you hear me? There is a way out. There is a way to live the lives we have in Jesus. Glorious, victorious, abundant, free, happy, and darkness free lives.

So, let's all put aside our differences, and grab hands, as we dive into the topics God has laid on my heart for us.

[10]

And this isn't me writing to you, it's me writing to *me* too. We're going to examine how to start making that terrible darkness of the enemy tremble, through the glorious light of Jesus Christ.

Chapter One

One **Solution** for all problems

Jesus said to him, "I am the way, the truth, and the life. No one comes to the Father except through Me."
John 14:6

As you know, there are many huge, and even more huge, problems in this world. Everywhere you turn. In our families, at our schools. We hear it on the news, it's on social media. It's everywhere. We can't get over one thing in our homes or elsewhere before something else comes crashing in like a tidal wave.

It may seem quite hopeless.

But guess what? It's not.

There is a Solution.

And it's not anything we can do or have done. The solution lies in a wonderful, loving God.

He's what this world needs.

He's what *we* need.

In the beginning God created a perfect world (Genesis 1:1). There was no cancer, there were no shootings, and there was no divorce. It was perfect. But God also created man with a free will. And man sinned with that free will. And then we were separated from God.

But God is a merciful God and He had a plan. Oh my, He had a plan. He sent His only Son Jesus Christ that we might live and no longer be separated from Him (John 3:16-17). He sent Jesus to die on a rugged, terrible cross, for *our* sins-not His sins-*our* sins. Jesus took on every pain and every sin and nailed it to the cross. He took everything you have or ever could feel and took it upon Himself. He died for you. Yes, for *you*. He saw *you* worth dying for. Yes, YOU. The one who feels worthless and unloved. Oh, don't ever think that; Jesus loves you so much that *He died for you.*

We need to get how powerful and wonderful this is. Okay, this is the Son of God. He was one with God, but He died a death fit for no man. The cruelest death ever, for *you* and for *me*. Oh wow, that's just amazing! That is just...wow! Praise Him!

So He took all our pain and He died on the cross. But you know what else? *He didn't stay dead.* Nope, death couldn't hold Him, and the third day He arose from the grave and defeated death! He arose from the grave alive and we have life in Him. We have life, people!

Jesus is everything good and right we could ever need.

He is Love: *But God demonstrates His own love toward us, in that while we were still sinners, Christ died for us,* Romans 5:8.

He is peace: *"These things I have spoken to you, that in Me you may have peace. In the world you will have tribulation; but be of good cheer, I have overcome the world."* John 16:33.

He is kindness: *And be kind to one another, tenderhearted, forgiving one another, even as God in Christ forgave you,* Ephesians 4:32.

He is happiness: *...for the joy of the LORD is your strength,* Nehemiah 8:10.

He is our Healer: *But He was wounded for our transgressions, He was bruised for our iniquities; The chastisement for our peace was upon Him, And by His stripes we are healed,* Isaiah 53:5.

He is comfort: *I will not leave you comfortless: I will come to you,* John 14:18 (KJV).

Savior and Servant: *"Just as the Son of Man did not come to be served, but to serve, and to give His life a ransom for many."* Matthew 20:28

He is everything right.

Now let me ask you this: don't you think God is the answer for all this hurt and darkness? Don't you think He can heal us if we turn to Him? Don't you think He is Light itself?

John 8:12 says this, *"...I am the light of the world. He who follows Me shall not walk in darkness, but have the light of life."* And John 1:5 says, *And the light shines in the darkness, and the darkness did not comprehend it.* Jesus is Light. He is Light itself. And let me tell you, no matter how much the devil tries, he can't overcome that Light.

Oh, Hallelujah!

Ladies and gentlemen, of every age, race, shape, and size, let's go to Jesus. He wants us. He died to have us. It doesn't matter what you've done, Jesus wants you. It doesn't matter how dirty you are, He wants you. And He can make you clean. And He'll make you new, if you'll let Him.

In Him we have redemption through His blood, the forgiveness of sins, according to the riches of His grace, Ephesians 1:7.

We have forgiveness. We have redemption.

Jesus wants you to hand Him your burdens (Psalm 55:22), He already carried them on the cross.

Come to Him, He wants to give you rest. "*Come to Me, all you who labor and are heavy laden, and I will give you rest. Take My yoke upon you and learn from Me, for I am gentle and lowly in heart, and you will find rest for your souls.*" Matthew 11:28-29.

He is peace. He is rest.

I pray that if you don't know Jesus as your personal Lord and Savior, you'll invite Him into your heart.

And, if we already know Him, we'll continue (or maybe begin) to accept all these truths about our Friend.

~~~~

If you don't know Jesus Christ, please pray this prayer down below. He'll change your life.

Jesus Christ, I'm a broken sinner and I need You. Please forgive me of my sins. And make me new in You. Thank You for dying on the cross for me. Thank You for taking all my sin upon the cross. Thank You for rising from the grave and giving me life! Here's my life, Jesus, make it new in You. Thank You, Amen!

Wow! Congratulations! Welcome to the family of God!

Yeah, that's another thing, when you get saved you become a child of God

(Galatians 3:26). We're all brothers and sisters in Christ.

The LORD is my shepherd; I shall not want.

Psalms 23:1

Chapter Two

The Holy Ghost

However, when He, the Spirit of truth, has come, He will guide you into all truth; for He will not speak on His own authority, but whatever He hears He will speak; and He will tell you things to come.
John 16:13

The Holy Ghost with the evidence of speaking in tongues is not something everyone believes in, or maybe even knows about. And the devil has tried to make me ashamed-I did feel ashamed and embarrassed-and I'm so sorry to God for that. But this is a wonderful, amazing gift that Jesus gives us after we accept Him into our lives.

The Holy Spirit is our Guide. He is our Comforter. He is straight from God, one with God, and gives us power and equips us. He dwells with us and is always there for us. The speaking in tongues is the evidence of this amazing

Spirit. Some people believe you can be filled with the Holy Spirit but without speaking in tongues. But I don't believe that and the Bible doesn't say that. In the Bible when someone was filled it says they were filled with the Holy Ghost, with the evidence of speaking in tongues: Acts 2:4, Acts 19:6.

In the Old Testament God would give His Holy Spirit to people temporarily for them to fulfill their duties, but it couldn't dwell in them until salvation came. (Psalm 51:11), but it wasn't something that dwelt with them always. But when Jesus came and was filled with the Holy Ghost it was with Him always (Mark 1:10-11, John 3:34). And John the Baptist, the prophet who came to prepare the way for Jesus, was filled from His mother's womb (Luke 1:15).

Now let's talk a little bit about what the Holy Spirit *is* and *does*.

Now before we get started, please do not think I'm a know-it-all in this, because I'm not. I'm so unlearned in this area and God is still teaching me.

~~~~

The Holy Spirit is a Comforter.

And I will pray the Father, and He shall give you another Comforter, that He may abide with you for ever, John 14:16 (KJV).

Now the first thing Jesus says about the Holy Spirit, when He started to teach His disciples about the Holy Ghost that would come when He was crucified, resurrected, and ascended to heaven in John 14, is that He is a Comforter. And He repeatedly calls Him this in chapters 14 and 16.

And let me tell you, He is a Comforter for sure. When you're stressed or upset and you ask Him for help and He brings a verse to your heart and mind that is just what you need...perfect. And when you just pray in tongues, it's so peaceful. *So know, He is a comforter.* And what a Comforter He is.

He is our Guide into all truth.

In John 14:17 Jesus calls Him the Spirit of Truth, and Chapter 16:13 He says this, *However, when He, the Spirit of truth, has come, He will guide you into all truth; for He will not speak on His own authority, but whatever He hears He will speak; and He will tell you things to come.* There, He calls Him the Spirit of Truth again. And He really is.

Ask and He'll guide. He's done it for me with writing, with trips, with friends and family.

When that big decision comes up, ask: He'll direct. When that boy or girl comes into your life and you wonder if this is the one, ask and He'll direct. When you're unsure of what a scripture means, ask, He will direct. Just ask with anything. Then, after you've heard Him, move forward.

He is a Teacher.

But the Helper, the Holy Spirit, whom the Father will send in My name, He will teach you all things, and bring to your remembrance all things that I said to you, John 14:26.

Okay, He's for sure a teacher and a reminder. When I'm going through something and turn to Him, and sometimes when I necessarily 'don't turn to him', He brings just the right verse, or something He's told me, to my

[22]

heart and mind. And peace enters my heart.

And a teacher. Lately I've just been in awe of the Holy Spirit teaching me things. It's like when I read and ask, the understanding just comes. I've never had such understanding before!

So, He'll teach you. Ask and seek.

When my Daddy was going to lay hands on me to receive the Holy Ghost, one of the things He said was that the Holy Spirit would give me a better understanding of the scriptures. And that is so true.

He is One with God and Glorifies Him.

He will glorify Me, for He will take of what is Mine and declare it to you. All things that the Father has are Mine. Therefore I said that He will take of Mine and declare it to you, John 16:14-15.

He is one with God and Jesus. And what He speaks and shows us is of Jesus. And in that way He glorifies Jesus.

The Evidence of Speaking Tongues.

And He said to them, "Go into all the world and preach the gospel to every creature. He who believes and is baptized will be saved; but he who does not believe will be condemned. And these signs will follow those who believe: In My name they will cast out demons; they will speak with new tongues; they will take up serpents; and if they drink anything deadly, it will by no means hurt them; they will lay hands on the sick, and they will recover." Mark 16:15-18.

As we said before, the tongues are the evidence of the Holy Spirit.

And this is our special prayer language. When you first start speaking in tongues, and maybe for a long time after that, you won't know what you're saying. But you know its power and it's special. And even when God may give you interpretation, it won't be every time you speak in this prayer language-unless God chooses to take you through a special season of that.

This is the evidence of the amazing gift God has given us.

We need to speak in it every day. We need to keep that gift active. It's so powerful.

~~~~

The Holy Spirit is a most precious gift that we should seek. God desires we have this gift. It's straight from Him. Don't we want something that is straight from God? We should at least desire the things of Him.

I encourage you to start exploring this in the Bible. Read John 14 and 16, and Acts 1 and 2. Want it. Seek out an anointed, godly person who has received this gift. Ask them to lay hands on you so you may receive. But want it people, want it.

The devil will try and make you ashamed, ashamed of seeking it and wanting it. And when you have it, he'll try to make you ashamed then too, and try and make you think it's not useful. But the devil is a liar.

The Holy Ghost is beautiful and I refuse to be ashamed of it.

And they were all filled with the Holy Spirit and began to speak with other tongues, as the Spirit gave them utterance.

Acts 2:4

Chapter Three

A personal relationship with Jesus

*I am the good shepherd; and I know
My sheep, and am known by My own.*
John 10:14

I really like the way Isabella
Morganthal puts this. In talking about a
relationship with Christ in her books *I
Dare You: Finding your passion and
lighting your world* and *Worth it All:
Running the Race of a Lifetime*,[1] she
illustrates it like getting to know your
best friend. You don't become best
friends over night. You hang out and get
to know each other. And you don't just
do all the talking; you listen to your
friend, as well
    This is a beautiful way to put our
relationship with Christ.
    The Bible says Christ is our Shepherd
and we are His sheep. Jesus says His

sheep *know* Him. So we, His sheep, should know Him like Christ says we should and like He knows us.

God created a soft breeze that feels so nice, He created the beautiful flowers that blow in a field or on the side of the road as you drive. He made you too. God deserves our trust and our life. He deserves us serving Him.

It's a privilege to serve Christ. It really is. It's beautiful to dive into God's Word and hear and see His heart. To see how He wants you to live, to hear God revealing special things to you. It's beautiful, Him giving you understanding. It's beautiful to have Him give you your own message out of a passage of scripture. It's beautiful when He reveals a calling on your heart through scriptures or speaking it gently to your heart.

If we want to know Jesus, if we want to know His heart and the way to live, we need to develop a relationship with Him. We need to develop a praise and prayer life. We need to take time to read the Bible every day. We need to take time to listen for His voice. Every day we need to do these things.

Below we're going to examine four things we need to do in having a personal relationship with our King.

The four things

1: Read our Bible.

It's vitally important that we read God's word. *"...Lord, to whom shall we go? You have the words of eternal life."* John 6:68.

Why should we read our Bible? The Bible is life; it's the words of life. Jesus is Life and the Word. And we need to feed off God's life. We need to follow Him. We need to read the Bible to know God's heart and His plan for us as Christians.

And God reveals special plans to us through His word. And, sometimes, He reveals special messages through a passage of scripture for us and a situation that it applies to in our lives. That's really special to me. And it's really special when He reveals unique lessons to you out of a verse or passage you wouldn't have thought contained something like that. It's wonderful! So, read God's word. It's life. It's refreshing. It's peaceful. It's awesome.

You know something else wonderful about God's word? It's powerful. And the devil can't stand a chance against it.

For the word of God is living and active and full of power [making it operative, energizing, and effective]. It is sharper than any two-edged sword, penetrating as far as the division of the soul and spirit [the completeness of a person], and of both joints and marrow [the deepest parts of our nature], exposing and judging the very thoughts and intentions of the heart, Hebrews 4:12 (AMP). We'll talk more about God's word against the enemy in *Chapter Seven.*

We need to *study* God's word too, not just read it.

Everyone has special things that work good for them in how they read and study their Bible. Some may learn and relate more if they write in a journal. Like writing verses down and ways they speak to you, and how you can live them out.

Sometimes taking a shorter passage and just writing verses and points down is so fun, and really helps you get in depth with it.

2: Praise and Prayer.

God created the heavens and earth. He created the stars and the sun. He created the seas and the trees. He created kittens and cute dogs. He created YOU. He created all life. He is faithful. He is a deliver. He is good. Throughout all history until now God has shown mercy to us. Even when we were rotten and turned away from Him, when we cried unto Him, He delivered and forgave. He made a way for Salvation through Jesus Christ and for us not to be separated from God-when we most certainly didn't deserve it. He's amazing.

My overall point? He. Deserves. Our. Praise. Yes, He deserves our praise. We need to lift our hearts and hands in worship to Him. We need to thank Him for His many blessings. Because, if you just think, He's given you so many. I really need to get better at just thanking and praising God for things like a warm bed, family, friends, laughter, cool breezes, food, my gifts and talents. But it needs to be heartfelt; it doesn't need to just be going through the motions.

And prayer. Prayer is so important. It's a way for us to talk to our God. We can talk to Him. Wow. That's pretty important and amazing if you think about it. We can talk to the God who made everything!

Something I like to do, and recommend, is I pray over what I read in the Bible. Like thank God for it or something He taught me out of it. It's a way to review what I read and acknowledge it.

And God wants you to ask Him your request. Pray for things you need. Pray and believe. Pray for you and your future, and the things God is calling you to. Pray for your friends and family. Pray for those who don't know Jesus to come to Him. Pray for healing for people that are sick. Pray for your teachers, the leaders of your country and state. Pray for those in slavery-pray for their freedom.

Here's good verses that sums up our topic. *Therefore I exhort first of all that supplications, prayers, intercessions, and giving of thanks be made for all men, for kings and all who are in authority, that we may lead a quiet and peaceable life in all godliness and reverence. For this is good and acceptable in the sight of God our Savior,* 1 Timothy 2:1-3. Being thankful first is so important.

Prayer is so powerful and may we all develop a prayer life. *And pray for one another, that you may be healed. The effective, fervent prayer of a righteous man avails much,* James 5:16. Jesus Himself had a prayer life. He prayed many hours and consistently.

Be anxious for nothing, but in everything by prayer and supplication, with thanksgiving, let your requests be made known to God, Philippians 4:6.

3: Listen.

Referring back to Isabella Morganthal's statement, you don't do all the talking-you listen. We need to listen to our Father. Oh, He has amazing things for you. Listen to His voice. Listen for His guidance and correction. Listen for that sweet voice, be still and wait for your Father to talk. *Be still, and know that I am God…* Psalm 46:10.

Jesus would go, pray-and most certainly listen-in the Bible, look at the amazing things that would happen afterwards.

4: Just Him Time.

Something my Daddy taught me is where you have a time that is just for Jesus. That you make it just about Him and not about what you need. I have this. It's like a time to praise God and watch/listen for Him to reveal traits about His character. It's simply beautiful and amazing! And I recommend doing this at some point in the day or week.

Motivation

Now don't get me wrong. I know motivation to get into the word and prayer can be lacking at times.

So here is a tip to make yourself do these very needful things.

I'm sure we all don't have much trouble getting on Instagram or Twitter. Or drinking our favorite coffee and watching our favorite TV show.

Something to do is, make a commitment that if you miss these things-spending time with Jesus-for no important reason you won't get to do other things. Like whatever you do the most of the things mentioned above, or things you do that weren't mentioned, don't do if you don't spend time with God. For instance, if you're a real Instagram person, no Instagram the next day if you don't read and pray. If you always get your favorite *Starbucks* drink on the way home from school or work, make a commitment you won't do that if you miss your time with your

Jesus. This is a discipline to help us get on the right track.

And if you're a parent, take time to help your younger children read some in the Bible. Maybe read some to them.

Something we do in our family, what we've always done, is my Daddy does Bible Time with us children every night we can. We sometimes work on a series of studies. He may read articles from himself (my Daddy writes and has a ministry), or articles from other writers. I've realized while writing this how special this Bible time is!

Family times in God's word are important too. Take time to have a Bible time in the morning (we used to do some in the morning too) or at night. Whatever time works best for you.

As for parents, I know that it can be hard to have that time when you have children and work. I've never been a parent so I can't necessarily give advice, but I would like to encourage you to try and find time to stay in the word and have a relationship with Christ.

Let's all try to discipline ourselves to stay consistent in God's word.

This is something I've not mastered yet or haven't worked on much; but we may have to say no to a friend and family about something in order to have that time with Jesus.

And I know, after awhile of feeding off the Word of Life, we'll grow and want to seek Him more-it's fun!

~~~~

Time seems to just slip away from you sometimes. Here are some ways to keep God's word around you, and in you, when you can't necessarily sit and read.

Now I can safely say most of us have a phone. YouTube or get BibleGateway, and listen to audio of the Bible as you drive, shower, and get dress. Write scriptures on sticky notes and stick them on your backpack, in your room, kitchen, and in your car. Read them as you go about things. Stop and reflect for a moment.

Listen to worship music or messages as you go about. Some people I like to listen to are Sadie Robertson, Emma Mae Jenkins, and Christine Caine.

But make sure that you don't skip out on personal Bible time because you can do these things. I recommend doing these things even when we have our time with God. Definitely have a personal Bible time every day, set that in stone. And let's make sure we don't leave God and what He's shown us in that time behind: take it with us.

~~~~

Something else we do need to remember is not to get into a rut. Don't make a relationship a religion. Yeah, just read that last sentence again.

We all have a problem of getting into a certain routine in how we do our Bible time and we can hardly do anything different. This can get in the way of the Holy Spirit leading. Let Him lead. Let's purpose to change our routines up some days. But of course let's always listen for the Holy Spirit to guide us in what we should be doing.

Before you start your Bible studies, pray. Ask the Holy Spirit to come, ask Him to teach you things you've never seen before. Ask Him to give you revelation and understanding. Invite His presence to come and be with You.

I hope we all have learned a few things about having a relationship with Christ. I know I have just writing this!

"And when he brings out his own sheep, he goes before them; and the sheep follow him, for they know his voice. Yet they will by no means follow a stranger, but will flee from him, for they do not know the voice of strangers."

John 10:4-5

Chapter Four

Forsaking worldly standards

And do not be conformed to this world, but be transformed by the renewing of your mind, that you may prove what is that good and acceptable and perfect will of God.
Romans 12:2

The world says we have to dress a certain way, be a certain way, have a boyfriend or girlfriend by a certain age, talk a certain way, and even pressures us to have sex by a certain time.

You know what we need, ladies and gents? We need to forsake the standards the world has set for us and start living out the standards Christ has set for us.

Fashion

You see, everything we do should be in line with God's word. How we dress should be according to what He directs us in His word.

Have your own style. Let's not copy someone else we think we have to dress like. We may be inspired by someone else's style and want to dress that style-but let it be *us*. Let it be *you*. Don't just do it because you think you have to.

You may want to be fun and copy some look from a movie, and that's okay too. As long as it's in fun and not because you idolize them.

I used to struggle, and still do sometimes, with idolizing movie characters. It would throw me into a panic mode if they **did** anything I didn't like, and I defended them if someone **said** something about them I didn't like. God delivered me from this, praise Him, and I am a lot better. It doesn't bother me as much to hear someone saying something unfavorable about movie characters I like.

So, while we can enjoy having favorite movie characters or music artist, let's not idolize them and let them become our life. After all, it's just a movie (speaking to me here), and music artist are just people.

So, if we like to be trendy and keep up with fashion-and it honors God-that's fine. Just don't do it because you feel peer pressured to.

Be YOU

The fear of man brings a snare, But whoever trusts in the LORD shall be safe, Proverbs 29:25.

A lot of us struggle with acting differently than ourselves around other people.

And sometimes it may be hard to discover what our true self is.

But with God, we can.

You are unique and have your own unique personality. And with God we can seek to live a life that is us, and have a God honoring character.

Solomon (the author of Proverbs) says in the verse above that the fear of men brings a snare. And he was the wisest man-besides Jesus-who ever lived. And He is so right. It brings all sorts of problems. Fear of being yourself, acting in an ungodly way because you're too afraid to stand up for what you believe. Hurting people you're close to because you change who you are to please people-and you may put them down to fit in. This kind of behavior can result in compromise and could, eventually, resort in forsaking Christ.

The only person you should worry about pleasing is God. And you need to stay true to Him and yourself. And if you are in Christ, staying true to Him and you, is really the same.

Let's seek God and ask His help in helping us not change when around other people, especially around unbelievers. With His help we can be confident in who we are and what we believe. Not changing to please people.

It's sad when people don't accept us or shun us. But Jesus chooses us and that's all we need.

Love

Love is a beautiful thing, and having a boyfriend or girlfriend is wonderful. But in God's timing and who He directs you to be with (We'll talk more about relationships in *Chapter Nine*). You shouldn't go around trying to find someone to be with because everyone else has someone, or because people are pressuring you to. And it shouldn't be because people make fun of you or look at you funny when you tell them you don't have a significant other. Like I said before, wait for God's timing.

And sex should be a holy and God honoring thing. And should not be something you're forced into, pressured into, or do just because you're a certain age now. It should be something that takes place when you're married and to someone you truly love.

Sex is beautiful and the world has drained its beauty into something ugly, with movies, books, and songs, ect.

God designed sex and has a plan for it and we all need to seek out in the Bible what His plan for it is.

So don't feel sex is something that has to come because of pressure. It's a beautiful thing that God designed for marriage and it's a more beautiful thing to wait, than to just do it because of another reason.

Partying

Partying, drinking, and carrying on in other ungodly ways is not God honoring. You can have good clean fun without all that. Seek to have fun in a godly way and unlike the world. You'd be amazed at all the clean fun you can have. Like a water park day with your family or friends. Play board games. Have karaoke parties or other fun parties. Watch a movie and eat loads of food (my siblings and I could tell you about that). Just let's make sure our fun is clean and in a way God smiles and says, "They sure are having fun and that pleases Me." Don't you think Jesus played with children and His disciples? They probably went swimming. He probably played tag. He probably played hide-and-go-seek with all the children that were around Him. HE HAD FUN FOR SURE! He knew how to be joyful in God and have loads of fun with the people around Him.

~~~~

We live in the world but we aren't supposed to be like this world (John 17:14-15). The devil is the king of this world. And we don't want to serve Him. He's all evil.

Sometimes it's hard to know the way. But thankfully we have Jesus. He's the Truth, the Life, and He is the way. We are to follow Him. Jesus directs and guides us (Luke 1:79, AMP).

James 4:4 even says this, *Adulterers and adulteresses! Do you not know that friendship with the world is enmity with God? Whoever therefore wants to be a friend of the world makes himself an enemy of God.*

I don't know about you, but I don't want to be an enemy of God. Do you?

Direct my steps by Your word,
And let no iniquity have dominion over
me.

Psalm 119:133

Chapter Five

Some sowing and reaping

Do not be deceived, God is not mocked; for whatever a man sows, that he will also reap.
Galatians 6:7

If we really considered this verse deeply we would probably be more careful of what we sow, and destine to live a more godly life. Like if we thought about all the disrespect we give and know we will intern get it back, we may try to be better little people.

In this chapter we're going to talk about sowing and reaping. We are also going to talk about the power of our words.

Jesus said in Matthew 7:2 this, *...And with the measure you use, it will be measured back to you.*

So basically how we treat others will be the way they will treat us. Like for instance, you may be rude to the lady in the *Stake-'n-Shake* drive thru all the time, and when you get a job at *McDonalds* a year later, everybody is so rude to you. You're reaping some seeds there.

When you're rude to your siblings or are a bad friend, don't be surprised when they're rude to you and a bad friend back.

Now I know that sometimes people are just rude to us. We live in a sin world. But let's make sure that when something seems to keep happening to us, we examine our lives and see if we're getting back what we gave. And when we realize this, let's repent and ask God for forgiveness. Strongholds, no matter how big, can be broken with Jesus.

Let's ask God to help us sow good seeds. If we accept His help and guidance, we can live a more godly life and start planting flowers instead of thorns.

Just think of it this way. Jesus says, *Therefore, whatever you want men to do to you, do also to them, for this is the Law and the Prophets*, Matthew 7:12.

Your words

And here's another powerful truth, your words are powerful. You can confess things over your life with your words. Think I'm strange, look at the Bible. *Death and life are in the power of the tongue, And those who love it will eat its fruit,* Proverbs 18:21.

Life and death are in the power of the tongue? Wow.

Here's an example: I used to say the word crazy a lot and a lot of people do this too. Like, "This drives me crazy." Or, "I'm going crazy." But after I went through a terrible time of torment in my mind, I started watching what I said-and how I said crazy. I don't know about you, but I don't want to be crazy one day. I don't want to be tormented in the way the devil has done to me. The way he's tormented me could definitely be considered him trying to make me crazy.

This may seem really ridiculous to some of you. You may be like, "Beth, that is ridiculous, you can't say something and it happen." Well, I didn't say it, God did. The devil feeds off those bad words, and he looks for ways to get us. Our words can give him room for death. Death, people. It can invite Him into our lives. But if we watch what we say and what we confess over our lives-and speak God's truth-we're feeding and sowing *life* into our lives.

We need to refrain from saying things like, "I'll have cancer when I'm fifty because my Dad died that way." Or, "I'll have heart disease because my Mom does." NO, NO, NO! God wants us to speak life, and more and more life! Jesus spoke life; we are to follow His example (John 14:12).

It may seem hard to realize that our words have power over our life and our future, but it's God's truth. And He doesn't want us giving room to the enemy.

We need to diligently watch the room we give the enemy. Strife, contention, bad entertainment, and music, and every evil work gives room for the devil to come in like a flood.

Let's sow good seed so good may return to us.

And like I said before, we live in a fallen world, so some things just come because of that. But let's examine our lives and hearts always.

Let's speak truth and only confess good things. The Bible says those who love it will eat its fruit.

Be positive. Not Negative.

"I am the vine, you are the branches. He who abides in Me, and I in him, bears much fruit; for without Me you can do nothing."

John 15:5

Chapter Six

R.E.S.P.E.C.T.

*Be kindly affectionate to one another
with brotherly love, in honor giving
preference to one another.*
Romans 12:10

Respect is so important. Respect for our parents. Respect for siblings and other family members. Respect for our bosses and co-workers. Respect for people in general, like the *Starbucks* employee.

Something we've gotten away from is respect. We are rude a lot of the time; we have no grace for people. We don't respect our parents or siblings, even just for the individuals they are.

And before we go any further, please don't think I'm an expert at this because I'm not. I'm a little unsure how to even write this.

But with the Lords help I'm going to write how we can be more respectful, and dive into what that means.

What does RESPECT mean?

Respect is admiration. It's high regard. We have no problem having regard for celebrities. Teens have high regard for Justine Bieber and older people have high regard for John Wayne.

If we can defend and give our attention to celebrities, how much more should we respect our parents and those around us. And God, we need a respect for God.

We need to pray for an honest and pure respect for God and people. God says to respect and honor people over our own selves (see verse at the beginning of the chapter).

God says to do unto others as we want them to do to us, and I think that falls under the line of respect too (Matthew 7:12).

So let's look into some examples of people we need to respect in our lives.

Some examples of RESPECT

God.
Okay, God deserves our respect. You might say, "I serve God, that's respect." It is, but it goes beyond that.

When you use God's name in vain, that's disrespectful. Very disrespectful. I used to do that all the time. I didn't cuss using His name, but I did it in exclamation or in irritation, ect. I'm thankful God broke me of this habit; God forgive me.

We don't need to make jokes about God. We need to respect and honor our Creator, who has truly done so much for us. He sent His Son to die for us, He took everything on Himself that belonged to us.

Know that the LORD, He is God;
It is He who has made us, and not we ourselves;

We are His people and the sheep of His pastures, Psalm 100:3.

Look closely at that verse and let it speak to your heart. He made us, not ourselves. He is God. He's our Lord.

Let's respect Him.

Parents.

"Honor your father and mother," which is the first commandment with promise." Ephesians 6:2. The Bible promises that we will have a long life when we honor our father and mother.

Our parents deserve our respect. They provide for us and take care of us, and just them being our parents demands our respect towards them.

I know it's hard sometimes, but may we all work toward a heart set attitude that desires, *and willingly*, honors our parents. I think we'll be happier doing so.

And, parents, honor your children. Respect them. Please. I think it's sad and unfair when parents don't do this. Children feel mistreated and upset when they feel they have to give all the respect. I'm not saying you aren't their authority, but please respect them as your children and other as human beings.

An overuse of authority isn't right either, even for parents (1 Corinthians 14:40).

Siblings.

I don't know if I ever thought about respecting our siblings until recently. But it's true, they deserve our respect. They're family and fellow human beings. They have dreams, desires, and hobbies we need to respect and be interested in. And we should do things with them too. It's so important to play games with your siblings and do special things with them. It's just so fun and important. Hey, watch *The Andy Griffith Show* (yeah, it's one of those old shows and my family's favorite).

Friends.

A friend loves at all times... Proverbs 17:17.

Friends deserve our respect, too. And I'm in no way the expert at this. With God's help, I'll get better.

We should destine to be the best friend we can be. We should keep up with our friends, check up on them, and invest in their lives. And just like our siblings, respect them for individuals. Be interested in their interests.

And if you're like me and have pen-pals and email pals, you aren't always the best at getting back to them ASAP. God spoke to me awhile back and told me I should be better at this. While, in no way I've conquered it yet; I totally need to. We need to appreciate and honor them enough to keep in contact and be a faithful friend. Make yourself available to them if they ever need someone to cry with or just talk to.

One of my good friends is good with that. When I'm going through things she offers to let me call her and cry with her. She knows she may not always have the answers, but she makes herself available for me to just have someone to let it out to.

Let's remember: a friend is a friend at *all* times. The good times-the bad times. They're always a friend and keep loving.

Our Teachers and Bosses.

Yeah, I'm homeschooled but I've heard those stories about public school teachers.

Sometimes it can be hard to respect them but let's strive to do that. Let's not be disrespectful in class and on our phones all the time. Let's try our best to learn.

Likewise you younger people, submit yourselves to your elders. Yes, all of you be submissive to one another, and be clothed with humility, for "God resists the proud, but gives grace to the humble." 1 Peter 5:5.

And with bosses. People complain about their bosses a lot. And I'm not saying all our bosses are fair or right, but let's try our best to respect them with God's help. He's our Strength (2 Corinthians 12:9).

To all people.

We complain a lot. We complain about the employee that gave us our *Starbucks* drink and didn't add the special thing we wanted. We complain if someone didn't smile at us right when we picked up our waffle fries at *Chick-Fil-A*.

We're all guilty of this.

Did you ever think that the man who didn't put your extra shot in your coffee was human and just failed to do so? I worked at a restaurant once for a fundraiser and you could easily get confused. Let's have some grace even though it's frustrating.

Did you ever think that the girl that didn't smile giving you fries maybe wasn't feeling well or lost a loved one that meant so much?

You see, we all go through things and we all make mistakes. It's important to have respect for the people we come across and have grace for them. Not to say we won't screw up, but God gives grace to us if we ask (1 John 1:9).

~~~~

We all need to be careful of having an attitude of *I don't like people*. I don't like it when I hear people saying this and it's wrong ya'll. People are people. And we are to love them, not get an attitude that we don't like them in general. Is that showing the love of Christ?

Sometimes it's hard

Yeah, it's hard to respect some people.

And some people don't deserve our respect. Some parents aren't good to us and don't even love us. And that's hard. Some siblings treat us like trash, and so do friends and people we come across.

Render therefore to all their due: taxes to whom taxes are due, customs to whom customs, fear to whom fear, honor to whom honor, Romans 13:7.

Some people don't deserve respect and that's when it can be hard.

Paul says in Romans 12:18, *If it is possible, as much as depends on you, live peaceably with all men.* It's not always possible to live peaceably. But as much as we can, let's try our very best. And sometimes distance may be the solution to chaotic and dishonoring situations.

If you're in a abusive situation, I definitely recommend getting out of that.

With God's help we can try our best and rely on His strength.

Let nothing be done through selfish ambition or conceit, but in lowliness of mind let each esteem others better than himself.

Philippians 2:3

Chapter Seven

Mind Torment, Anxiety, and Depression

The thief does not come except to steal, and to kill, and to destroy. I have come that they may have life, and that they may have it more abundantly.
John 10:10

    The devil is a tormenter and a thief, just as Jesus says he is. And Jesus is life and more abundant life.

    I think anxiety is one of the biggest things you hear about people struggling with. And a lot of it reverts back to a mind thing.

    I've struggled with anxiety and mind torment. Boy, the devil has tried to get me. And he's trying and getting so many other people.

~~~~

Something the devil really gets people with is their *mind*. He has me. He's really tried to destroy me. And I know commonly He gets people with thinking they're not good or pretty enough, or that we don't measure up. And even with sexual lies.

But what I've learned about the devil is he is a liar (John 8:44). And what I've also learned is Jesus is truth.

The devil has tormented me with so many lies. When he began to really try and take my life was in 2016. He came at me with so many lies. It was so bad I'd go take a nap to get away from it. It was a sad time to go to sleep at night and just hope that when you woke up the thoughts were gone. Only to wake up to them greeting you.

But something fantastic I learned was to fight against the enemy. Once I went, knelt, praised, prayed, and read my Bible-I was better by Christ. But this was only the beginning of the battle.

I started to fight against the enemy, really fight. Later I told my Momma and eventually my Daddy knew. And God used them to teach me more.

If you're ever going through something don't let the devil tell you not to share it with someone. Just opening up with someone and talking to them is so helpful. And talking to spiritual leaders will help you get godly advice and direction. Ask them to pray over you and rebuke the devil with you. When the army of God starts rising up, the devil will have to shrink.

Something that turned out amazing from that junk was I started becoming serious about my relationship with Jesus. Praise Him!

So, I began to fight, and fight hard. The devil came at me in every direction. Making me feel guilty of past wrongs. It was a long, hard fight. He'll come hard, you know, but Jesus will come even harder.

By Jesus Christ I am free. Praise YOU, JESUS!

And you know, even just recently the devil has tried to get me with some of those lies in opposition to this book (the devil doesn't like you obeying God at all; he opposes God's word on every side).

Anxiety was another thing the devil tried to get me with, as he does with so many.

For quite some time when it got toward evening I would get anxiety in my stomach. And even before that, when the dogs would bark or something, I'd be afraid of someone coming to murder my family. Or terrorist breaking in.

This was torment indeed, like the anxiety that gets so many people. Anxiety is a disorder even if you don't have a severe case. It's fear, plain and simply. And it's from the devil. But you know what; he can be defeated by Jesus. Wow, Praise God!

How my journey of freedom started was in our family Bible time, my Daddy was talking about facing fear. It was that night I knew I had to face the fear in my life. The night was a fear-the feeling that something would happen at night was a fear. So, I walked outside around my house, quoting scripture. Jesus was by my side and I faced the night.

I kept doing this over and over again.

When my *real* breakthrough finally happened is when I text my Daddy and asked if we could take authority over the spirit of fear as a family. The devil still got me with fear, even though I was better. So we took authority over fear. But before we did, my Daddy said how what people are afraid of aren't really things to be afraid of-like someone breaking in your house. He really enlightened me that night. So we prayed and the anxiety was lifted! And I continued to face the fear and became freer and even freer. Praise HIM.

~~~~

Depression is something many people sink into, and the devil tried to get me with too. It was hard for me to smile and be happy for awhile. Depression is awful.

And the saddest thing about this, and the anxiety and mind torment, is when people won't seek help for these things. When they don't accept the power God has given them and rise up like the children of God they are and fight. Saying, "Not today, Satan. Not today."

Depression can come from failed relationships, lost loved ones. I've seen both these happen with my family members and it's sad.

It can come from bullying or listening to the devil's lies. You may be tempted to give up. To end it all. But please, dear one, know you are so loved and cared for. Jesus loves you beyond measure, and those aren't just words. It's a true reality. Please listen to this and seek help. And above all, seek God's help. He has such an amazing plan for you. He wants to use you. He wants you!

The devil doesn't want you alive, he wants you to end it all and not do anything for God. He wants suicide rates up.

Defy his odds.

Rebuke that lie, that demonic spirit. It will flee.

Ask God to deliver you. We need to ask Him to heal us-with any torment. Ask His healing. Seek godly counseling; don't be ashamed to seek help.

~~~~

You may be wondering right now, "What do you mean, Beth, fight against it, use the power God has given you, quote scriptures?"

Well, let's let Jesus tell you what I mean.

How to fight and win

Then Jesus was led up by the Spirit into the wilderness to be tempted by the devil. And when He had fasted forty days and forty nights, afterward He was hungry. Now when the tempter came to Him, he said, "If You are the Son of God, command that these stones become bread." But He answered and said, "It is written, 'Man shall not live by bread alone, but by every word that proceeds from the mouth of God.' "

Then the devil took Him up into the holy city, set Him on the pinnacle of the temple, and said to Him, "If You are the

Son of God, throw Yourself down. For it is written: 'He shall give His angels charge over you,' and, 'In their hands they shall bear you up, Lest you dash your foot against a stone.' "

Jesus said to him, "It is written again, 'You shall not tempt the LORD your God.' "Again, the devil took Him up on an exceedingly high mountain, and showed Him all the kingdoms of the world and their glory. And he said to Him, "All these things I will give You if You will fall down and worship me."

Then Jesus said to him, "Away with you, Satan! For it is written, 'You shall worship the LORD your God, and Him only you shall serve.' "

Then the devil left Him, and behold, angels came and ministered to Him (Matthew 4:1-11).

Okay, so pay close attention to this story. At this time Jesus has been baptized, filled with the Holy Ghost, was almost ready to begin His ministry, and then He's led into the wilderness to be tempted of the enemy.

So the devil starts in on Him, telling Him to do this or that, using scripture to try and trick Him. And every time the devil came, do you see what Jesus does?

He quotes the scripture at him. He defies the devil's lies with God's word.

The devil comes back and back again, but what does He do? He quotes the word of God. And then, what does it say? *Then the devil left Him.*

So, you see, God's word will defeat the enemy. God's truth will defeat the enemy.

Jesus took mind torment, anxiety, and depression on the cross and He defeated this work of the enemy. And He has given us weapons to fight against the enemy. His word, His truth (which is the word too), and authority. He died and rose again, and He's given you weapons, Warrior, to fight against the enemy of your soul who loves to see you down. Who wants to see you destroyed. Who doesn't want you doing anything for God!

He took it all but you have to accept it, and receive what He's given you.

Luke 10:19, *Behold, I give you the authority to trample on serpents and scorpions, and over all the power of the enemy, and nothing shall by any means hurt you.*

The devils were subject unto Jesus, He commanded them to leave and they left (Luke 4:33-36). And Jesus said that the works He did we could do also. And even greater works because He died, rose again, and went to the Father. Like wow, even greater works than Jesus! Whoa!

So in Luke 10:19-when Jesus says He has given us power-seventy people, whom He had given authority to, had went out and ministered to people. The devils listened to them and they cast them out, through Jesus' name.

The devil can't resist the word of our living and powerful God (Hebrews 4:12). He can try and keep coming and even take a bit to leave. But. He. Will. Leave.

Start quoting scriptures at the devil, resist him, and cover his nasty lies in God's beautiful truth. That's something I learned from *Sadie Robertson*, to speak out the lies.[2] When I did this and then covered them in God's truth, it was an amazing deliverance for me. So say out loud to the devil the lie He's bothering you with. Say it's a lie. Then say, "But God's truth is this: who Jesus sets free is free indeed."

2 Corinthians 10:5 (KJV) says, *Casting down imaginations, and every high thing that exalteth itself against the knowledge of God, and bringing into captivity every thought to the obedience of Christ.* When the devil comes against your mind, when he says you're not good enough, say loud and clear at the enemy this verse.

Start meditating on the word of God and replacing the devil's thoughts with God, and good thoughts. *Finally, brethren, whatever things are true, whatever things are noble, whatever things are just, whatever things are pure, whatever things are lovely, whatever things are of good report, if there is any virtue and if there is anything praiseworthy—meditate on these things,* Philippians 4:8.

When fear comes quote 2 Timothy 1:7 with confidence, choosing to accept what God has given you and not the enemy! *For God has not given us a spirit of fear, but of power and of love and of a sound mind.*

When depression comes say (personalize it), *'Fear not, for I am with you; Be not dismayed, for I am your God. I will strengthen you, Yes, I will help you, I will uphold you with My righteous right hand,' Isaiah 41:10.*

And say, *He who is in you* (ME) *is greater than he who is in the world,* 1 John 4:4.

You have power, dear ones, and victory doesn't come overnight always-that's a special miracle if it does. But fight and keep fighting, knowing Jesus is before you and behind you (Psalm 139:5). Keep fighting knowing Jesus has already won on the cross. You just have to exercise and believe what He's won for you. Victory is there if you take it!

And in some cases, medical help may be needed. You may need to seek Christian counseling and physiology. But I firmly believe God is all able. He is a healer. Christian YouTuber *Savannah Lewie* was healed of depression with God-without medication.[3] Hallelujah!

So don't be afraid to seek help. And even when medical help is needed, still fight against the enemy. Getting medical help doesn't exclude all this. Don't exclude God's word, because it's what's going to get you through.

And speak in tongues against the enemy, pray in your spirit language. See how long he can resist that. Speaking in your prayer language is so sweet and beautiful.

One thing I think is so special is this verse. *Please read this verse closely and let it speak to you life.*

And Jesus came and touched them, and said, **Arise, and be not afraid.** *And when they had lifted up their eyes, they saw no man, save Jesus only,* Matthew 17:7-8 (KJV).

Fear will leave when we look steadfast towards Jesus.

When the disciples looked up, they saw *no one* but Jesus. That's what we need to do in times of fear...look steadfast toward Jesus. Not the fear, not the people around us, just Jesus.

Don't give place to the enemy

We also need to remember not to give place to the devil (remember *Chapter Five*). *Nor give place to the devil,* Ephesians 4:27. When we give place to him and his works, we build up strongholds in our lives that we may suffer with sooner or later. Like for instance, when I was afraid of someone coming and killing my family, I realized the root of this was me watching a movie where someone came and shot someone's family at night. I had planted a seed and was suffering from it. So if you're struggling with fear or just any torment, examine what you're letting in and have let in the past. If you're struggling with sexual lies and are watching sex movies, that's a stronghold and a seed you're reaping. Same with fear, if you're watching horror movies and having fear, that's a result of a stronghold. But with Jesus those can be torn down! *For though we walk in the flesh, we do not war according to the flesh. For the weapons of our warfare are not carnal but mighty in God for pulling down strongholds,* 2 Corinthians 10:3-4.

Even strife and not living Christ-like can open room for the devil to come in with sickness and all manner of problems.

And I know that the devil tries to get us even if we haven't given place to him in certain areas.

And some people can handle certain things others can't. Like my mind has been something the devil has gotten me with, so I have to be extra careful with what I let in. Same goes for you; whatever you know the devil tries the most to get you in-whatever is a weakness in your life-be extra careful you guard against it.

But in any case, what we're watching and doing should all be clean and appropriate. I don't think it's in any case right to watch sex and horror things, though, or listen to it. Horror movies are demonic and give place to the enemy big time, and not just horror movies are demonic either. And sex is a private and beautiful thing, not to be put on movie screens. Let's pray and ask God to show us what is right and wholesome. I love clean stuff. It's the best!

Let's examine ourselves always, and when the devil comes, let's see what's in our life that may be giving the devil free range. Then let's start tearing down those strongholds. Get rid of those things and start building up Jesus strongholds. Those of faith, love, and only letting godly things into our lives.

You are Royalty

But as many as received Him, to them He gave the right to become children of God, to those who believe in His name, John 1:12. You're royalty, ladies and gents. Sons and daughters of God. Don't let the devil trample over you. You're royalty, highly chosen, and highly favored. God calls you His and calls you His child. You are above the lies of the devil. Use the height God has given you.

Don't let your royalty and all God has given you be wasted.

When we're fighting with God, and being the warriors He has called us to be, we can say mind torment, anxiety, and depression is not us. We won't let the odds be so high for these torments. We'll be a generation, young and old, saying, "Not today, Satan."

Spiritual battles in general

The devil is after you. He's after you big time. He'll try and make you fall away or give into something not right. He may just torment you to the point you think you can't take it.

These are spiritual battles.

Every Christian has spiritual battles to fight. And while these may not be the most fun thing to do, if we trust God and fight with Him, He'll turn it around for good.

He does not bring temptation on us. He doesn't bring hard times. The devil does. He's the thief. God's the Shepherd.

What we've talked about in this chapter is just three examples of spiritual battles. There are many others. And we have to learn, through Christ, how to discern these and be prepared. But a lot of the times, though, things hit as out of nowhere and we're like...

Jesus said that if the master of the house knew when the thief was coming he wouldn't have suffered his house to be broken into (Luke 12:39). This applies to our spiritual battles watch too, I think. Watch so you'll be in tune with the Holy Spirit so you can avoid situations that could lead to letting the devil in. Watch, so when the attacks come you can use God's weapons and fight, and win. And your house won't be destroyed.

Just remember, there is a word of God to defeat every lie of the enemy. Search out scripture, it's there. And there are many verses that go with many situations!

Let's be prepared. Let's be fighters. It's hard to face so many battles, but through God we're victorious and He is our Strength.

Sometimes you may get discouraged

Sometimes you may fight, and fight again. You may be better one day then feel despair again the next day.

One night I got so overwhelmed and discouraged. I was so mad, and maybe a bit angry at God. I didn't understand why I wasn't better. I had cut off everything-social media, ect. While I was better some days, I didn't understand why I wasn't well completely yet.

While I was going through this, I listened to a message that helped me-along with a number of other things. This message was by *Keith Moore*.[4] And he helped me realize that it wasn't that God wasn't helping me, because He certainly was and had, it was that the devil wasn't dead. And the devil wasn't going to stand by while I did what God wanted me to. He was going to try and stop me.

Don't ever feel like God has forsaken you.

He hasn't. He's right there, giving you strength to fight.

Jesus did help me.

He helped me every day and it's a shame that I forgot that for awhile.

Know that if the fight goes on and on, it's not because God has forsaken you...it's just because there is an enemy after your soul. He'll try and stop you for living for God. But press on, even when you don't feel strong, because it's Jesus' strength you have to rely on anyways. You can't do it alone.

Therefore submit to God. Resist the devil and he will flee from you.

James 4:7

Chapter Eight

Judging

Judge not, and you shall not be judged. Condemn not, and you shall not be condemned. Forgive, and you will be forgiven.
Luke 6:37

We are too quick to judge instead of show mercy.

We judge what people are wearing, their Christian beliefs that are different from us.

We don't need to go making hate videos on people, or start talking about someone who isn't dressed as modestly as we believe.

People, we can disagree with someone or not approve with something, without going on and on about how terrible it is. If you see someone has a problem, pray for them.

Did you see Jesus meeting someone in the Bible and saying, "Oh, um, you're showing too much cleavage, and I think I'm going to go tell everyone I know how immodestly you are and talk about it for the next two weeks."

You see, we can hate sin, and speak against it, but in a loving, kind way. Jesus, when He spoke and taught us something, it was in love. Utter love.

There may be a time you may need to make a video and address something. And as always, you shouldn't approve of sin. But our witnessing and such should be done in love, and not in a judgmental way.

Sadly, we have given Christ a bad name by judging and not loving people. We've made Christianity a religion when it's really a personal, loving relationship. God never meant for it to be religion, and it's sad we've slapped Him in the face by making it so. People don't want to be Christians because they don't want to be judgmental.

We even shun Christians when they do wrong, and hurt them to the point where they don't want to come back to Christ.

If someone divorces, the church sometimes shuns them because they say they're sinners and adulterers. We hurt people. And they don't want to come back to Christ because of the way His people have represented Him. People judge Christ by what they see in us. Jesus said we are the light of the world, and we are to shine before men (Matthew 5:14-16). We are Christ's representatives. *Now then, we are ambassadors for Christ, as though God were pleading through us,* 2 Corinthians 5:20.

Let's represent Him right. And the overall way to do that is love.

When we judge it should be with God's standards and what is right.

We need to, with God and His word, judge what is right and wrong. With God's Holy Spirit we need to discern the way of God.

We may need to examine what is in people, people we're following and looking up to. We may need to see if it's something we should be following. We may have to judge a situation and determine if it's God's way.

In our family and friend's lives if we see something that needs taken care of, as our responsibility as a good family or friend goes, we may need to kindly mention it to them. But don't try to change people or always be pointing out their wrongs. Remember, we can give kindly advise (in some situations, ask God for direction, we don't need to open our mouth about everything) in love. We'd be better to seek God and let Him work on ourselves than trying to fix everyone else. Jesus said we can't help anyone else without first helping ourselves (Matthew 7:3-5).

There is a difference in judging and being judgmental. Look up the definitions; there is a difference. A good judge in court judges a situation and renders a verdict, without being judgmental of the people.

Remember, what you sow you'll reap. What judgment you give others you'll get back.

Jesus judged the Pharisees because they criticized everyone else. You go around being critical; you'll get judged for that.

Mercy triumphs over judgment. *For judgment is without mercy to the one who has shown no mercy. Mercy triumphs over judgment,* James 2:13. Show mercy. Mercy **will** return to you. I'd rather have mercy shown to me than judgment.

A new commandment I give to you, that you love one another; as I have loved you, that you also love one another. By this all will know that you are My disciples, if you have love for one another."

John 13:34-35

Chapter Nine

Relationships

He who walks with wise men will be wise, But the companion of fools will be destroyed.
Proverbs 13:20

There are many relationships in our lives. Family relationships, friendships, and romantic relationships. And we should strive our best to be the best we can be in all relationships.

We talked a lot about relationships in *Chapter Six*, but, while we'll dive a little deeper into family and friend relationships, this chapter will be devoted mostly to romantic relationships.

But as in regards to family, we should be the best daughters and sons we can be. Confiding in our parents and being open with them. I've not always been the best at this, still aren't, but it's something I should work towards. As should we all.

We should be respectful and obey them, even when we're passed eighteen and are still living at home. Just because we are an adult now doesn't mean we shouldn't be respectful. But even when we're gone from our house, we should always listen to our parents and consider their advice.

And regarding our siblings, instead of being so centered on our friends and social life, we need to invest in them. Play games with them; do fun things with them that they like. My parents always say that your sibling will be the ones that will always be there. And that's true.

Let's strive to see how important these relationships are. And let's not go away from the close relationships we make when we all get older and go our own ways. This had been a fear in my life, but I will destine not to let it be a fear, and rather work on not letting those ties slip away.

And sadly, even though sometimes we try to invest in people and stay close connected, we don't get a response.

I know a lot of people don't have good family situations. They live in divorced families, and have step-siblings they're not close to. God has blessed me with a good family position. But I know broken family situations can be hard and I pray that God will heal and restore.

You know, something God showed me was that the devil is after the family.

Listen to what Jesus said would happen in the last days…and if you think about the family situations you see around you, you'll see that this is happening.…

"Father will be divided against son and son against father, mother against daughter and daughter against mother, mother-in-law against her daughter-in-law and daughter-in-law against her mother-in-law." Luke 12:53.

Don't you see this is our families and the families around us?

The. Devil. Is. After. Our. Family.

I know this first hand with how he's come against my family.

He wants to stir up strife. He wants to see us quarrel and for bitter rivals to fester between siblings.

Remember what we talked about in *Chapter Five* and *Chapter Seven,* about giving place to the devil? Well, this applies to this too. When we let the devil in our homes with strife, confusion, and hate...he'll gladly come in and set to destroy our families.

And he's so satisfied when our families are being destroyed.

Ladies and gentlemen, every person around the world, don't make the devil happy.

Seek to make peace with your grandchildren you don't have much to do with.

Work if at all possible to reach to out to the grandparents you don't have relationships with.

Make peace with your siblings.

Make peace with your parents.

Let's not be one of the families that at the end of the world are destroyed...but rather are tied together so tight-no wind could break it.

Romance

Pretty much all of us want that romantic love. We want that boy to love us, that special girl that's just ours. But somewhere along the way love has gotten to be all out of sorts...from loose sex, to heartbreak, to jealousy and lies. It seems to have just gotten completely out of hand.

We need to get back to God's standards and what He has for love.

I think love is beautiful and I know God loves love. After all, He's the inventor of love. I don't think people realize how much He truly *loves love.*

He has a plan for love and for us. If we give Him our future in that area and surrender to His will, it will be beautiful.

I think with our love life in God hands He can do wonderful things with it.

Below let's look at what God says love is and does.

~~~~

Love suffers long and is kind; love does not envy; love does not parade itself, is not puffed up; does not behave rudely, does not seek its own, is not provoked, thinks no evil; does not rejoice in iniquity, but rejoices in the truth; bears all things, believes all things, hopes all things, endures all things. Love never fails. But whether there are prophecies, they will fail; whether there are tongues, they will cease; whether there is knowledge, it will vanish away... And now abide faith, hope, love, these three; but the greatest of these is love, 1 Corinthians 13:4-8, 13.

This sums up love.

Let's look closely. Love is kind; it doesn't envy, does not behave rudely, does not think evil, rejoices in truth, believes and endures all things. And it doesn't fail. Everything will cease, but true love doesn't. Out of faith, hope, and love, *love is the greatest.* And something else I like; *it's not provoked.* Look up the definition. How much love does this today?

How much better would love be if we carried what **true** love is into it. Look at these things. They outweigh distrust, cheating, and failed relationships.

If God says this is what love is, shouldn't that be the way we behave in love?

Nobody likes breakups or failed marriages.

Shall we purpose to have a right relationship and give our love life to God? I know I will.

Now let's look at some things we can do to have better relationships in our life.

~~~~

1: *Give it to God.*

It would be a whole lot better if we put our romance in His hands, surrender to His will, and let Him do a perfectly good work. I gave this area to God and I'm going to let Him do His thing. *Casting all your care upon Him, for He cares for you,* 1 Peter 5:7.

And believe me, it's not easy. I've struggled with looking around and trying to find my own man…but with God I'm going to be free of this. I'm going to let God bring him to me. I'm tired of looking.

2: *Wait for the one He brings and in His timing.*

But those who wait on the Lord Shall renew their strength; They shall mount up with wings like eagles, They shall run and not be weary, They shall walk and not faint, Isaiah 40:31.

This is even hard for me to get. There are so many failed relationships it's hard to imagine being successful with the one person God brings to you. But with God we can, that is His plan. He's not interested in us giving all our time and energy to different relationships, and then them failing and us being left broken and miserable.

So wait, wait until God gives you the go. When someone comes into our lives and we find ourselves liking them, let's pray and ask God's direction. Let's see if it's His will for us to pursue a relationship with this person. When we hear God say yes, and we go forward listening to His guidance, we'll be happy and the relationships will be successful.

3: *Be okay with being friends.*

A man who has friends must himself be friendly, But there is a friend who sticks closer than a brother, Proverbs 18:24.

Getting to know each other, really know each other's hearts and convictions, is so special and so important. When you may not be in a relationship officially yet, and you're just talking and getting to know each other- seeking where God leads-just being friends is just right.

And even after, when you're official (and married), still get to know each other. How hot she or he is not going to hold a relationship together. It's God and hard commitment. A lot of people set too much stock on how sexy she/he thinks you are than their heart being after Jesus.

4: *Set boundaries.*

Let all things be done decently and in order, 1 Corinthians 14:40. It is a person's heart that truly matters. Don't make the relationship about physical touch. Seek God and know what you feel He's directing you to set for your boundaries.

But when it comes to sex, that is something beautiful, and that is something God designed for husband and wife. It's something special and holy. And it's for marriage. *Marriage is honorable among all, and the bed undefiled; but fornicators and adulterers God will judge,* Hebrews 13:4. Do we want to be judged for having sex wrongly?

When we have sex in this pleasing way to God, it honors and glorifies Him. Isn't it a beautiful thought to honor God with this, rather than giving it away loosely? It's beautiful to even think it honors God, when done in His design.

Set boundaries, have people who will keep you accountable. Do group activities as well as one-on-one time. Avoid situations that could lead to temptation.

Having sex wrongly can result in all sorts of turmoil. Pre-marriage pregnancy can bring many problems. Custody arguments, going in and out of courts all the time. Never trusting the other one, and not having your child all the time. And all in all, it damages your child and gives them a bad example. And they're caught in the middle. And before all that, it can lead to abortion...

God knows what He's talking about when He wants us to do it His way. We all can admit it's better for us and for our future.

5: Listen.

My sheep hear My voice, and I know them, and they follow Me, John 10:27. Listen for God, all during the relationship, even through marriage. Listen for guidance and correction. You may be going too far or letting your focus be on the wrong thing.

I heard a testimony of a girl who had a great relationship, but God asked her to give it up because she was putting all her trust in it.[5] So listen, and follow His voice. Don't worship that relationship or put your contentment in it. Jesus has to be our contentment. We can put it in others, but we'll only end up hurt. People fail, but God never does.

We need to keep our focus straight. Remember, the commitment we're making is the most important thing-*not* how much we can touch or how much sex we can have when we're married. Getting married just for sex is not a good reason, or a good intent, to get married at all.

6: Don't be unequally yoked.

Do not be unequally yoked together with unbelievers. For what fellowship has righteousness with lawlessness? And what communion has light with darkness? 2 Corinthians 6:14.

Decide right now that you will not be with someone who is not a born again believer, and who does not have the same values as you. I've seen so many problems in relationships because they weren't equally yoked.

Sometimes couples are both believers and just believe so differently. One wanted to be pure and the other didn't, and then there was compromise. I've seen relationships like this fail. God had a reason for saying it; you can't go through life with divisions.

Commit to God and destine to be *equally* yoked with someone. Believe God for someone who believes Him and has the same beliefs you are convicted to have. And most importantly, the convictions God wants you to have. Someone may come into your live that helps you have better convictions. Just be open to God.

7: Don't settle.

For you were bought at a price; therefore glorify God in your body and in your spirit, which are God's, 1 Corinthians 6:20.

Don't. Ever. Settle. When the waiting get's long, don't settle. When it seems there isn't a Christ-like person out there, don't settle. When she/he is a great Christian person but they want sex, don't settle.

Don't settle for a man that is looking at pornography and cheating on you that way.

You are bought with a price; the special price of Jesus' blood. To settle for anything less than His best would be unfair and sad, and so degrading on you…and Him.

Waiting, no matter how long, will be worth it in the end. Just you wait and see. And if you don't believe me, look up *Jamie Grace*.

8: Don't lust.

Jesus said just looking on someone to desire them is adultery (Matthew 5:27-28). Let's not lust.

We don't need to look at someone and desire them or think lustful thoughts toward them. That person is someone's spouse; may be yours, may be someone else's.

So, in the same way you want someone keeping their eyes off of your someone; do the same to the opposite sex you come across. That person is going to be (or may be already, be careful of how you start thinking about random people you come across-people you don't know yet) someone's spouse one day. Honor that and respect it. Same way you want it done to you.

9: Pray.

Pray. Pray for your future spouse. Pray for your future together. Pray for their life right now. Always pray. Prayer is so powerful.

~~~~

I know sometimes relationships fail, and that's sad. Especially in the times we live in now. Jesus said in the last days that the love of many would wax cold (Matthew 24:12).

I know sometimes we think we have peace and hear God's voice and go forward. Then the person we are with comes out to be a jerk and we're left broken.

I know there are abusive relationships and marriages we have to leave.

I get all that. We live in a fallen world. And the devil is rampant. And one way he gets us is with our relationships.

But I know when we place our trust in Christ; there are better options than what's in this world.

Let's refocus what we're listening to about relationships and just focus on God's advice. Seek encouragement from people who are waiting too. Seek advice from godly people who are in tune with Him and have gone before you. Seek out a godly couple who lives an example of Christ' love. Seek

Christian counseling before you're married, and even after if there is a problem. But most importantly, put your trust in God, and only Him; not the relationship itself.

And I know we all make mistakes, but I believe God will forgive anything and make you completely new like He says He will (2 Corinthians 5:17).

And I know sometimes we are forced into sexual activities and are abused in that area. And we feel shamed or like it's our fault. We feel we can't be pure.

That. Is. Not. True. When someone forces you into something, it's not your fault.

And let me tell you this: you're a priceless human being; no one can take away from you what God has given you. Without Him, none of us are innocent. Hear Him whispering how *precious* you are to your heart. Let His words of truth sink in. He says you're of more value than many sparrows, who doesn't fall without God seeing them (Matthew 10:29-31).

A warning

Now here's a little warning. Should a relationship fail and you be done wrong-don't take on a rock heart. I've seen people (the ones I've seen are women) who have gotten so hard towards men in general, because one man did them wrong. They get this attitude that they won't be hurt again and that men are all jerks. They get an attitude that they're better than men in the relationship and men are gullible-and sweet things are cheesy now. I've even heard them say love doesn't exist.

Please, ladies and gentlemen, don't get this attitude. I know when we're hurt we can get angry, and hurt others because we're hurt. But let's turn to God instead of bitterness. He heals. It won't happen overnight, but He will heal. *...And by His stripes we are healed*, Isaiah 53:5. Let this little truth sink into your heart.

...Weeping may endure for a night, But joy comes in the morning, Psalm 30:5.

~~~~

With God's help we can become the generations that suffer long with love, that are kind and trust, and that never fails.

Who's with me?

"But from the beginning of the creation, God 'made them male and female.'
'For this reason a man shall leave his father and mother and be joined to his wife, and the two shall become one flesh'; so then they are no longer two, but one flesh. Therefore what God has joined together, let not man separate."

Mark 10:6-9

Chapter Ten

Body Image

"Therefore I say to you, do not worry about your life, what you will eat or what you will drink; nor about your body, what you will put on. Is not life more than food and the body more than clothing? Look at the birds of the air, for they neither sow nor reap nor gather into barns; yet your heavenly Father feeds them. Are you not of more value than they? Which of you by worrying can add one cubit to his stature?

"So why do you worry about clothing? Consider the lilies of the field, how they grow: they neither toil nor spin; and yet I say to you that even Solomon in all his glory was not arrayed like one of these. Now if God so clothes the grass of the field, which today is, and tomorrow is thrown into the oven, will He not much more clothe you, O you of little faith?

"Therefore do not worry, saying, 'What shall we eat?' or 'What shall we drink?' or 'What shall we wear?' For after all these things the Gentiles seek. For your heavenly Father knows that you need all these things. But seek first the kingdom of God and His righteousness, and all these things shall be added to you.
Matthew 6:25-33

In this passage Jesus is saying for us not to worry about our needs, just not to worry about life basically.

How many of us do you think worry about our body and how it looks?

How many of us compare our bodies to celebrities or models, or just those around us.

I haven't heard about men doing this like women, but they may struggle with looking masculine, ect.

Either way we struggle with body image, it's wrong and sad.

People, we put such a stock in the shape of our bodies. Are butts aren't big enough or our breast too small. We starve ourselves to try and obtain a certain body. We compare ourselves and envy the bodies of others. We feel down when we see another *perfect* body. We worry no man will want us or they'll be disappointed in us.

This is all so wrong.

We need to see what Jesus says about this, because He does have something to say.

Listen to this closely; this is in Matthew 10:29-31, *Are not two sparrows sold for a farthing? and one of them shall not fall on the ground without your Father. But the very hairs of your head are all numbered. Fear ye not therefore, ye are of more value than many sparrows (KJV).*

Wow. Jesus knows the *very* number of hairs on your head. And if you have a lot of hair like me, that's an extra big deal. The creator of the whole universe calls you valuable. The One who made everything and has all power. What more do you need?

You know what else He says about you, and what the Psalmist knew when he wrote this? *I will praise You, for I am fearfully and wonderfully made; Marvelous are Your works, And that my soul knows very well,* Psalm 139:14. You are *fearfully* and what? *Wonderfully made.* And the writer says that his soul knew that very well. Let that truth sink so deep into our hearts that we know that very well too. We are *wonderfully* made. *Wonderfully.*

You're a beautiful young woman, truly beautiful. And to the men out there, you're handsome.

Now don't get me wrong, it's a good thing to exercise and keep ourselves in shape. But not because we don't feel good enough or are comparing ourselves. Or because we're trying to look like our favorite celebrity, or trying to get a girlfriend/boyfriend. Don't sell yourself cheap by thinking you have to attract someone with your body. The right person will love you for who you are, and I'm positive they'll love your body too.

When we take care of our bodies in a healthy, good way, we will have the perfect body. And that's truly *perfect.*

Let's be confident in who we are and in the God who made us.

Let's erase the lies of the enemy, speak God's truth against him, and walk forward like the kings and queens we are. Who's with me?

...You are of more value.

Matthew 10:31

Chapter Eleven

Love *vs.* Hate

And walk in love, as Christ also has loved us and given Himself for us, an offering and a sacrifice to God for a sweet-smelling aroma.
Ephesians 5:2

Let me ask you this question. What sounds better, love or hate?

Jesus says that the world would know we are His disciples by our love. How many of us are loving? Or how many of us are being haters?

How many of us are bullies?

Sometimes the biggest way you can be a bully is with your words-I think it is the biggest way.

It's time we learn to accept people who are different from ourselves. You'll be hard fetched to find many people who are just like you or believe the same as you. It's time we quit being bullies to each other.

Bullying is a terrible thing. Some people intend to be bullies, and some are just mean accidently with their words-not realizing what they are doing.

We need to watch what we're doing and saying to each other. We need to stand up in love for the people in our schools, homes, and jobs who are being misused. Yeah, we may suffer with losing friends and popularity at school when we stand up for the girl who stutters. You may lose your job when you stand up to your boss, and you may lose your family when you stand against wrong.

But you would have gained so much more by showing love and doing what God wants you to do.

The overall thing is we need to show love all around. We need to hold our tongues and love, instead of being hateful. Remember all we talked about in being respectful? Apply that to this too.

We need to listen to those who have special needs and be their friend. Show love. I need to get better at listening to people.

Let's not get on social media and degrade each other, and post hate comments. Let's not get on social media and start complaining about songs we don't like or videos that didn't suit our fancy. Or call people names and talk bad about their looks.

Let's quit attacking police officers, but rather respect them and be ever so grateful for them.

Sometimes when we're hurt, we hurt back. We hate because we've been hated on. But God says this, *But I say to you, love your enemies, bless those who curse you, do good to those who hate you, and pray for those who spitefully use you and persecute you,* Matthew 5:44. Jesus loved the very people that crucified Him (Luke 23:34). How much more should we love those who hurt us?

Sometimes, it's not easy at all. Boy, is it not easy. But it's what God wants. And He's our Strength!

Let's show love like He says. He stresses the importance of this in the

Bible. He shows us His love and how we should love. That's the way people will know we're Christians! If they don't see anything different in us, how will they want Christ?

Let's appreciate people instead of putting them down. We need to support our police officers instead of bullying them on social media and shooting them in the head for no reason.

Remember the verse we read in *Chapter Five*? In Proverbs 18:21? *Death and life are in the power of the tongue…*

What you say to people can bring them up so much that they want to soar, or it can bring them down to where they want to die. Which would you rather speak to people? Life or death?

May we all get on our knees today and ask forgiveness for hate. We should ask God that He grant us love and patience for people. Let's apply 1 Corinthians 13 to our whole life.

And as always, ask the Holy Spirit for help, He's there for us. He really is! He showed me this when I was stressed and overwhelmed once. The Holy Spirit

is there to be our Guide, if we let Him.
Let's let Him.

*In this the love of God was manifested
toward us, that God has sent His only
begotten Son into the world, that we
might live through Him. In this is
love, not that we loved God, but that He
loved us and sent His Son to be the
propitiation for our sins.*

1 John 4:9-10

Chapter Twelve

Social Media

But the fruit of the Spirit is love, joy, peace, longsuffering, kindness, goodness, faithfulness, gentleness, self-control. Against such there is no law.
Galatians 5:22-23

What's your favorite social media? Mine's Pinterest and Instagram, probably. But I think Instagram and Twitter is a real favorite of a lot of people.

Socials are fun. But they can be time consuming or rob us of real life.

Does this make them bad or make it where we shouldn't use them?

No.

Social media is okay, as long as it is used in a God honoring and clean way.

Now, let's look at four simple steps we should keep front stage when using social media.

1: *God honoring and encouraging.*

Everything we do should bring honor and glory to God. So whatever we're doing on social media should honor God. And we should use it as a way to encourage people. It's okay to have fun and post funny things. Letting people have a great time and laugh in a clean way is encouraging, as well.

But always make sure it's Jesus honoring.

2: *Don't let it be the majority of your time.*

Are we spending the majority of our time on the phone? Are we never going outside to see God's creation or spending time with our family? Or are we letting the internet replace God?

Do we want to get to the end of our life saying all we did was be on social media?

Phew, not me!

Spending all our time on a phone or devise is such a waste. Never getting off and *actually living* is such a waste.

Lately God has helped me get better with this. Praise Him. But I'm not perfect at it.

I want to encourage us all to make sure we're cutting back on how much time we're on our phones. I challenge us to actually live and realize what waste it would be to live your life glued to a lifeless screen.

And, for you who have major ministries on social media, you may require more time.

3: *Watch what you're following.*

Our following and saves should be God honoring. What we're feeding on is so important, and what we're involved with reflects our character to others. We want to represent Christ well. And don't take me wrong, I don't think we should be people pleasers. Some people are always going to have a problem with what you do. We just need to let our characters reflect Christ well and let our light shine. We want a pleasing imitation of our lives for Jesus (1 Corinthians 11:1).

4: *Don't let it be your life.*

This is similar to step 2, but yes, don't let it be your life. Live a life that loves Jesus and fulfills His calling. Don't be so obsessed with comments, likes, and with what everybody else is doing.

Don't follow people so you can compare yourself, or so you can know everything the celebrities are doing. Don't follow for gossip.

Social media drains you if you're on it too much. I've had that in my life and seen it in others. Feeding yourself with the internet so much can make you sink into depression too. All that can have an impact effect on you.

There is so much going on in the world. And while we should be informed, our focus shouldn't be on all the wrong, but on our Jesus instead.

Remember Galatians 5:23? Self control, this is the key.

With the help of the Holy Spirit we can all use social media's and just internet in general, in a right, God honoring way.

Who's in?

So teach us to number our days,
That we may gain a heart of wisdom.
Psalm 90:12

Chapter Thirteen

God's calling for YOU

Therefore, brethren, be even more diligent to make your call and election sure, for if you do these things you will never stumble; for so an entrance will be supplied to you abundantly into the everlasting kingdom of our Lord and Savior Jesus Christ.
2 Peter 1:10-11

God has a calling for *you.* He has a calling for *your* life. He has something *wow* He wants *you* to do for His Kingdom.

Jeremiah 29:11 says, *For I know the thoughts that I think toward you, says the LORD, thoughts of peace and not of evil, to give you a future and a hope.* Jesus thinks thoughts toward you. He thinks thoughts of peace and not of evil. He thinks thoughts of *hope.* And *to give you a future.* Jesus has a future for you. He has a marvelous plan for your life. He has a special plan for **just** *you.*

Who has saved us and called us with a holy calling, not according to our works, but according to His own purpose and grace which was given to us in Christ Jesus before time began, 2 Timothy 1:9. Jesus has called you into a holy calling, not according to what you can do or have done, but according to His purpose. And He'll equip you and make you strong in His calling.

Now *we're all* called to share the Gospel of Jesus Christ (Mark 16:15), we are all called to do that. That's the number *one* calling that is on every believer's life.

But Jesus has given us each *special* callings and ways to further His Kingdom. And all these point to Him in some way.

Now Jeremiah 29:11 said *He knows the thoughts He thinks toward YOU.* Who? Y.O.U.

Please get this. Jesus has a calling for YOU. Think really deep about this. God, the maker of the *whole* universe, the

One who made pretty eyes and blue skies, *called you.* Wow. That's amazing God has a calling for all of us. Are we going to follow it?

How we know our God given callings

"Ask, and it will be given to you; seek, and you will find; knock, and it will be opened to you. For everyone who asks receives, and he who seeks finds, and to him who knocks it will be opened." Matthew 7:7-8.
It's that simple. Seek. Knock. *Listen.* Seek God and ask Him what His calling for your life is. And listen, listen for His voice. Watch for ways He may reveal this plan to you.
It's so simple. Seek and you'll find.
And those are words of Jesus, so they're for sure legit.

Age is a lie

Are you 6? Too Young to make a difference.
Myth.
Are you 12? Still too young.
Myth.
Are you 16? You need time be a teenager before you hit 18 and have to adult.
Myth.
81? Already lived your life. It's time for you to sit back and let the younger folks take care of doing God's work.
Myth.
People, age is a lie.
A lot of people fall into the lie of thinking they can't do something for God because they are too young.
That. Is. Not. True.
Age is a lie. To tell yourself that you can't do something for God because you're too young or because you've already been there and done that-IS A LIE. Straight from the devil who is the father of all lies.
Don't believe me? Look at the Bible.

Young people that did amazing things for God

Josiah.

Read his story in 2 Kings 22-23:1-30, and 2 Chronicles 34-35.

Josiah became King of Israel when he was *just eight years old.* And he did amazing things for God. At that young age he began to seek God. When he was just 12 he started getting rid of idolatry in the land. Later on, around the age of 25, he started repairing the Temple. And when the book of the law was found and read to him, he was heartbroken that Israel hadn't been keeping the law. When God saw he was humbled before Him, He told Josiah He wouldn't bring evil upon Israel (because they had turned from Him) while Josiah was still alive. Later, Josiah committed to seeking God with His whole heart. He also had the Passover kept in a beautiful and wow way that had never been kept before, and hasn't been kept like that since.

David.

Read his story in 1 Samuel 16-31, 2 Samuel, 1 King 1-2:12, and 1 Chronicles 11-29.

He was a teenager and he slew a giant (you've probably heard of him). He trusted in God. He had great zeal against someone who would defy the armies of God, (1 Samuel 17:26). When he saw the giant, he boldly volunteered to go face the giant...when everyone else was afraid. He didn't say, "I can't do this because I'm just a teenager, and he's awfully big. And I'm not old enough for God to use me." No, he went forward knowing God was with Him. He went boldly. The Israelites beat the Philistines that day. And, oh, he slew that giant.
You know something else about David? Even before he slew the giant, God called Him to be King of Israel (1 Samuel 16:13). David, a shepherd boy, was called at a young age to be king.

David was also an anointed musician. When he played his harp for Saul, the current king who had an evil spirit on him, it left him, (1 Samuel 16:23).

David went on to live a pleasing life to the Lord. He had a heart after God's! He was a warrior. He was a winner. He was a writer. He became King of Israel at the age of thirty. And from his family came Jesus Christ Himself. Wow!

I feel like David's whole life is so relatable to all Christians. Read the Psalms, it shows struggle and praise to God. He expresses God so beautifully and true.

Older people that kept on doing it

Moses.

Read his story in Exodus, Leviticus, Numbers, and Deuteronomy.

He was a mighty Prophet of God. He was a prince of Egypt and was going to be the next Pharaoh but he counted God greater riches than all those in Egypt-and Egypt ruled the world during that time. He was the voice God used to deliver the children of Israel from bondage in Egypt. He wrote the first five books of the Bible. He wrote the law of God. It was to Him God delivered His Ten Commandments.

And you know what; he kept on doing it until he died. He didn't decide, "Well, since I'm old and done a lot, I'll let one of these young Israelites do it. Because I'm old, been there, done that. I think I'll lay back and relax and let someone else lead these people."

NO. NO. NO. He kept doing it until he took his last breath (Deuteronomy 34:7). And he was 120 when he died. So go figure.

Elijah.

Read His story in 1 Kings 17-22, and 2 Kings 1-2:11

Elijah was a mighty Prophet of God. He lived boldly for God in a dark, dangerous time. God took care of him in many ways. He fed him when he was in the desert, and comforted him when he felt all alone. And God used him to make a mockery of the devil and his priests. Hallelujah!

And you know what? You're right, you guessed it. Elijah didn't quit doing God's thing until he died (2 Kings 2:11).

You see, these two people didn't quit when age came upon them; they kept on doing the things God called them to.

~~~~

Older people, please don't underestimate your impact on the world. I recently have gotten to know this older woman and I just enjoy being around her. It makes me happy to have someone I can go chill out with.

Young people need you. They need your encouragement and wisdom.

And I get it, some young people don't give a dime about older people and they hate hanging around them. Well, that's sad. But serve where you can and be there for them. You may be older in years but just invite a young person over to chat or eat ice-cream. Or maybe watch some television (old TV shows are my favorite but I know some young people don't like that) with them. This is so special and important.

Let's, young people, cherish the older people in our lives too. Maybe hanging around older people is easier for me because I've grown up around a lot of people that weren't my age. Maybe for teens that are just around teens being around older people, being friends with them, would be harder.

I was once in the mall and this girl was on her phone while her Grandma was talking to her. It appeared she was hardly listening or paying attention. And it came to me how she should listen to her Grandma. She would appreciate her more if she was gone. I know I do. I lost my Grannie when I was sixteen and I wish she was still here. I cherish her a lot more now that she's gone. It'd be nice for me to go over and watch westerns with her again.

Why don't we young people quit being brats and spend time with the older people we know. Really, it's quite fun. And they need it. How would you like to be old and feel alone with no one to hang out with or talk to? How would you like to know your grandchildren hate you? They need us and we need them. Let's start acting like the children of God we are and step into the fun and blessing we can give and receive from older companionship!

And if you don't have a grandchild or grandparent, seek out and watch for opportunities to invest in non-blood relationships.

That's the way it is for me and my new friend. And hey, we are *the party girls* (in a clean, fun type of way).

The Story of *my* dreams

Ye have not chosen me, but I have chosen you, and ordained you, that ye should go and bring forth fruit, and that your fruit should remain: that whatsoever ye shall ask of the Father in my name, he may give it you, John 15:16 (KJV).

This scripture really tells it for me in God calling me to *sing.*

From a young age I knew God wanted me to be a <u>missionary</u> and mainly to Columbia, South America. I've been privileged to go on three mission trips with an organization called *Eight Days Of Hope.*[6] The first one being in 2014.

But something that I was attracted to also at a younger age was <u>singing</u> and music. But that was something I was *way too shy for.*

I used to be really shy and was even too shine to read a scripture verse in church-for just my family and my Grand-G! I would shake and literally dread it for the time leading up to it. It was bad.

And I went through a time in life where I was doing something I wasn't supposed to with music, against my parents will. It was also a time I was really wondering what else to do with my life. I knew there was something else God had for me besides being a missionary, but I was confused as to what that was.

After watching the movie *Grace Unplugged* again, I sat on the stairs of my home, praying to God. I knew God wanted me to sing, I felt it. But I was too afraid to admit it was God; I was too shy for this.

I think when I really surrendered to God in this was on a walk (I confessed to my parents later), there I repented of my sins and *surrendered*.

Surrender is the key ya'll.

Praise my King!

I kept the calling to myself for about a year and then told my sister which later led me to tell my family. Then I started singing in church, and it got easier and easier. Now's it's so much better and easier for me to sing. And guess what?

I'm not so shy anymore. I can be shy but....

You see, God turned it all around. He turned a nasty situation into something for His glory and revealed His calling to me.

What the devil means for evil God can certainly turn it for our good.

And you know what? I thought there was nothing meaningful or anything that could minister to someone in this book with me sharing the story of my dreams. But God showed me it could help someone who thought they were too shy, too shy to do what God was calling them to. So you see, if you think you're too shy, too small or too insignificant to do that *something* for God, know it's a lie. When we are weak, He is strong. And we can do all things through HIM. *I can do all things through Christ who strengthens me,* Philippians 4:13.

Don't listen to the lies of the enemy. He opposes God's word and if God is telling you to do something, he'll oppose it. He'll tell you why you *shouldn't* and *couldn't* have heard from God. He'll tell you you're not good enough. He'll lie to you. But don't listen to him and go for that dream with a whole heart for God. Knowing He is truth and the devil is a liar. And if the devil keeps bothering you about a word from God, it's a for sure sign that it's from God. Because He doesn't want you doing things for God. He's rammed me hard about this book; it just shows me God has something wow.

And share your story. *It may just impact someone.*

Something else God has called me to is *writing.* This came along for me in 2013, but I really started giving it to God when I wrote my book *The Shield* in 2016-January 2017. I have two blogs. One is a ministry blog where I write articles from my heart, and the other is a life blog where I publish my Blog Book-*It's a Choice*-chapter by chapter (and other things too). And January 21st of this year I published my first book, *the SHIELD series.* All the Glory to God.

God has been good to me and I cherish and enjoy the talents He has given me. Praise Him.

And while I can sing 90 percent more comfortably in church, the thought of reading verses isn't my favorite but hey, God is God.

The same God that called me will call you. Just ask Him.

Be faithful in tiny things

He who is faithful in what is least is faithful also in much; and he who is unjust in what is least is unjust also in much, Luke 16:10.

What we have to remember in our callings is to be faithful in small things. Things don't always burst into *megas* right away.

Jesus said if we are faithful in small things, we'll be faithful in bigger things.

And sometimes things may just be "little" to the world. But if you did what God said, and helped just **one** person, than it's a mega impact.

But be faithful in what God has for you right now.

If it's your dream to be a missionary to South America but you haven't made it there yet, make the steps to serve those in your home and around you.

I want to be a missionary, and I really want to go overseas. But I've not made it there yet and I'm almost nineteen years old. I know I'm still young...but I've waited roughly eight years.

But you know what I like to do, I like to take up mission trip opportunities I can do right now. Like *Eight Days of Hope*. And things like #8doh are mission trips, and ones I'm happy to do!

So look and ask God for direction in what you can do now.

If you want to be a writer but aren't able to publish yet...keep writing anyway, all the time praying and asking God's direction.

If you want to be a singer...create a YouTube channel and sing now. Sing in church. But always ask God's direction.

Be faithful.

Recently I was a little disappointed in the 'success' of my first book, *the SHIELD series*. God had told me to *believe* and that He was going to do something great. But the sales weren't what most people would call successful.

But God showed me that this was being faithful in the small things.

My first book may not be successful in the world's eyes…but it's what God gave me. And while it may seem in a way small, it was God's gift to me and to others.

I'm awed of what God has done and what people have said about my book. People have told me it's their favorite novel, and it helped them follow the dreams God had for them. And the responses I got on the release day, and later, was not exactly what I expected. It was more.

So yes, this is epic and big to me.

Being faithful may not be easy…but even Jesus had to wait to begin His ministry until He was in His thirties. **It'll be worth it.**

He who calls you is faithful, who also will do it.

1 Thessalonians 5:24

Chapter Fourteen

Jesus is a Healer

Who Himself bore our sins in His own body on the tree, that we, having died to sins, might live for righteousness—by whose stripes you were healed.
1 Peter 2:24

Jesus is a healer. He healed an innumerable amount of people in the Bible. And He has all throughout History. He's healed me-and my family members.

Something I think we've forgotten is that *God heals*. He still heals as He always has.

We put our faith in doctors instead of Jesus. We don't take the time to actually trust Jesus anymore. Don't get me wrong, I appreciate doctors and they do a lot. God has used them to save my Father's life. I have nothing against the medical field at all; I'm just saying we have to get back to knowing God heals. And trusting Him to do so.

Sometimes we may get comfortable in a place we're in and don't want Christ' healing.

But people, Jesus took our healing on the cross. By. His. Stripes. We. Are. Healed.

Let's start receiving that again instead of settling on cancer or heart disease. Let's that receive He heals our broken hearts. Let's claim God's promises. Let's claim God's healing. Jesus has paid the utter price. We don't have to carry around sickness anymore! Hallelujah!

Let's not settle when we can soar higher and higher with Jesus Christ' blood.

Let's start trusting God again to heal our broken hearts and lives.

Believe

Sometimes we may pray and pray, and sometimes it may seem like its not working. Sometimes so much doubt may creep in while we're trying to have so much faith. *And sometimes it may seem hopeless.* Something God taught me during the process of publishing my first book, *the SHIELD series,* was to **believe**. Doubt and worry would start to creep up and what I was always reminded of was to *believe.*

And He showed me something very similar when a situation arose in my life that threatened to tear someone from me-who I truly loved.

Below are two (to name two) verses God used during both these times.

While He was still speaking, some came from the ruler of the synagogue's house who said, "Your daughter is dead. Why trouble the Teacher any further?" As soon as Jesus heard the word that was spoken, He said to the ruler of the synagogue, "Do not be afraid; only believe." Mark 5:36.

Now to Him who is able to do exceedingly abundantly above all that we ask or think, according to the power that works in us, Ephesians 3:20.

In the verse above, when Jesus says to only believe, Jairus-a ruler of the synagogue-had come to Jesus asking Him to come heal his daughter. She was *just twelve years old* and just about ready to die. On the way to heal her, a huge crowd followed and pressed into Jesus. And Jesus even stopped to talk to a woman who had touched the hem of His garment and received healing. While He was standing there talking to this woman, someone came from Jairus' house saying his daughter had died and not to trouble Jesus anymore.

Now look at Mark 5:36 again.

Jesus immediately says, *"Do not be afraid; only believe."*

He's saying that to us now. *"Don't fear. Believe in me."* When you pray and pray, and the cancer doesn't seem to be leaving, *"Don't fear. Believe in me."* When you're in pain every day, and it doesn't seem like God is showing up, *"Don't fear. Believe in me."*

And when it seems hopeless. Look at Ephesians 3:20 again. *Now to Him who is able to do exceedingly abundantly above all that we ask or think, according to the power that works in us....*

Jesus is *able.*

He is able to do it *exceedingly* and *abundantly.*

And He's able to do it *above* what we ask or *even think.* And if you have a big imagination, that's like....

And I can testify of that. Jesus did above what I thought in both the situations I mentioned. The person who was threatened to be taken away from me, is still here. My book is published. This is God.

He will do this for you, too.

Smile and believe in your God, knowing He's going to work it all out. He's going to heal.

The devil may just be taking a while to leave.

And, if Jesus is waiting, He's planning on doing something even bigger than you think.

Believe, don't doubt and *don't* give in to the devil, knowing it's going to be great in the end.

Jesus will come through.

Surely He has borne our griefs
And carried our sorrows…

Isaiah 53:4

Chapter Fifteen

Betrayal

"I will never leave you nor forsake you."
Hebrews 13:5

Have you ever felt betrayed and replaced?

I have and it hurts. It hurts badly.

When I was still in the ruff stages of this hurt I was seeking for someone who knew what it felt like. I wanted to ask strangers and I wanted some advice, desperately.

And once while I was crying, Jesus spoke to me and told me He knew how it felt. Jesus knew how it felt to be betrayed....

I'm sure a lot of us have felt betrayed and replaced. I'm sure a lot of you know that terrible, sad, wrenching feeling. That feeling of sitting there and watching someone else be in the place you thought was supposed to be *your* place.

Whether we've felt this with family, friends, or significant others, it hurts. And we may not want to face it.

But when we've been hurt we need to face the grief and let our emotions out to God. A good friend told me during this process that I had to face the grief. I had to face whatever it was that hurt me. This has helped me a lot and is so true.

If you're running from it, stop and turn to face it. When I did this, it helped a lot.

Cry out to Jesus who knows. He knows how it is.

You might say, "I know Jesus took all my pain on the cross and felt it all but it's so hard to grasp." Well, think of it like this: He felt betrayal before He went to the cross too.

Judas Iscariot was one of Jesus' disciples and he betrayed Him to the Pharisees, the people that had Him killed. He was Jesus' friend and disciple, and had been with Him for over three years. But he betrayed Jesus to His death (Matthew 26:47-50).

And Peter, Jesus' other disciple, denied that he even *knew* Him (Matthew 26:69-75). And all Jesus' other disciples ran when He was arrested. They forsook Him.

That's betrayal.

He had close friends betray Him. One to have Him *killed,* the other denying *they even knew Him,* and the other forsaking Him.

Jesus knew what it was like. He showed me this. He knew what betrayal felt like, *...A Man of sorrows and acquainted with grief...* Isaiah 53:3. And He carried that to the cross like He did everything else and nailed it there! Hallelujah.

It may be hard for you even to be comforted and grasp this reality; it is for me. I need to grasp this special revelation God has given me and let it comfort me.

We can be free from this hurt.

It can be a long and hard process, but we have Jesus who is a Healer.

Don't expect healing overnight, but accept the peace and healing God gives.

And let the pain out. When I truly started having a breakthrough is when I truly cried. I felt like I couldn't before, but I did and God is healing me now.

It still hurts sometimes, and sometimes I go to excuse it, but I have to remind myself that I was hurt. So don't try and act like it's not there, you'll only be faced with it again and realize you're still broken. But rather embrace forgiveness (I know it's hard), embrace freedom and joy-which God so richly gives. He's holding you always.

Sometimes people didn't mean to betray us or hurt us. They didn't mean to replace us. And, sometimes, they're really sorry. Judas and Peter were very sorry. Peter sobbed when he realized what He had done. He was very, truly sorry.

But sometimes we won't always have the person that replaced us sorry or even admit they did it. We won't have them coming and giving us an apology. A lot of the time, we have to forgive even after they haven't come to us and tried to make it right. Sometimes we have to accept an apology we never got. And that's hard. And while I don't have all the answers, I do have one.

And that's God.
Go to Him.

…And lo, I am with you always, even to the end of the age." Amen.

Matthew 28:20

Chapter Sixteen

Rush

Therefore, since a promise remains of entering His rest, let us fear lest any of you seem to have come short of it... Let us therefore be diligent to enter that rest, lest anyone fall according to the same example of disobedience.
Hebrews 4:1, 11

Life can be rush, rush, rush. And we can rush right along with it.

But what we shouldn't rush in is our time with God.

We should take the time to be still and know He is God. We need to give Him the courtesy of our time with Him and not let our mind wonder to all the other things we have to do.

Now I can let my mind wonder while I'm with Jesus, and I can get restless and get fidgety about something else I need to do. I can even get excited about the projects He's given me to do and get distracted with those.

We need to calm down, and not rush. We need to be still and rest in Him. He's Life and we need to dwell and feed off His Life. We don't need to be somewhere else in our mind.

Our time with God should not be something that is rushed, but rather something we settle unto and let the Holy Spirit move **on** and **in** us.

One of my favorite things to do is just lay back and think on God. To be still. This came from confusion and not knowing if I was doing everything right in His time. He showed me it was okay to be still when I thought I had to be moving a lot and raising my hands. Don't let your relationship with God turn into a bondage. Be *still*...that's what the Bible says (Psalms 46:10).

It's wrong and sad for us to rush our time with God when He's Life and He desires we know His heart. He desires we praise Him.

We may have to rush other things, but let God not be one of them.

One time God showed me that people were in a hurry to leave His presence. That's sad. We should crave it. I try now to calm my hurried little self and dwell in Him.

Sometimes we may not have as much time to do Bible time, but the time we do have-let's not rush. He deserves that time and much, much more.

You know, sometimes we may have to hold other things off to just be with Jesus. To rest at His feet and know He's all we need. His words are what we need to hear. Look at this story....

Now it happened as they went that He entered a certain village; and a certain woman named Martha welcomed Him into her house. And she had a sister called Mary, who also sat at Jesus' feet and heard His word. But Martha was distracted with much serving, and she approached Him and said, "Lord, do You not care that my sister has left me to serve alone? Therefore tell her to help me." And Jesus answered and said to her, "Martha, Martha, you are worried and troubled about many things. But one thing is needed, and Mary has chosen that good part, which will not be taken away from her." Luke 10:38-42.

Martha was so busy and wanting to get everything done. She was a worrier-like a lot of us. But on the other hand, her sister was sitting at the feet of Jesus-when there were things to do.

And Jesus *commends* this. He says Mary had chosen something that wouldn't be taken away from her.

Dirty houses will be taken away. Money will be spent. But the time we spend with Jesus, won't be.

"The grass withers, the flower fades,
But the word of our God stands forever."

Isaiah 40:8

Chapter Seventeen

Accepting Jesus' Sacrifice

Blotting out the handwriting of ordinances that was against us, which was contrary to us, and took it out of the way, nailing it to His cross; And having spoiled principalities and powers, He made a shew of them openly, triumphing over them in it.
Colossians 2:14-15

This article (with edits) was written for my Sunshine Girl *blog on October 11th, 2016. All scriptures in this article are taken from KJV.*

But He was wounded for our transgressions, He was bruised for our iniquities: the chastisement of our peace was upon Him; and with His stripes we are healed, Isaiah 53:5.

Guilt has a way of creeping up on us, doesn't it? I know it does me. But by God's grace, I know I'll overcome. Recently I was struggling with guilt over something I had done. It was long in the past but remembering it....

But God spoke to me in that time, "Is My sacrifice not worth more than this?" This is something I remind myself of now when things start to get at me. People, Jesus died on the cross for us! He took all our pain, all our torment, and through this sacrifice we can overcome! *And they overcame Him by the blood of the Lamb, and by the word of their testimony... Revelation 12:11.* So, are the things that get thrown at us in life more than what Jesus did? No, it isn't. Jesus' blood covers it all.

And from Jesus Christ, who is the faithful witness, and the first begotten of the dead, and the prince of the kings of the earth. Unto Him that loved us, and washed us from our sins in His own blood, Revelation 1:5.

How much more shall the blood of Christ, who through the eternal Spirit offered Himself without spot to God,

[155]

purge your conscience from dead works to serve the living God?
Hebrews 9:14.
What Jesus did is worth so much more than junk in our lives!
So trust in that. Believe that. When things creep up on you, remember His sacrifice. Remember how much it's worth. Remember that He died so you can be forgiven! Trust in that. Tell the devil, "Jesus' sacrifice is worth more than **your** junk." Make sure and let the devil know it's **his** junk, not yours. Don't claim it.
Smile and overcome.
So, let's remember His sacrifice.

~~~~

This is a precious thing God revealed to me, and something I remind myself of and try to hang onto now.
Think about this; it's so powerful.
Think of all Jesus went through, think of Him being slaughtered and hung on a cross. Think of Him being whipped and spit on. And think of feeling every pain in the world at one time. Imagine every

pain you've felt, emotionally and physically, and then imagine every other kind of pain you've heard about. Then imagine one person feeling it all.

And then try saying, "Nah, wasn't worth enough. I'm not going to accept His sacrifice and overcome."

People, when we choose to get under the enemies lies, when we choose not to accept peace and healing, we are saying what Jesus did for us WAS NOT ENOUGH!

Think about it. Ask yourself, "Is it enough?" Is it enough to believe God will heal your best friend of cancer? Is it enough to rise from depression and step into peace? Is it enough to forgive and let go? Is it enough to love the unlovable? Really ask yourself. Is it e.n.o.u.g.h.? Really enough.

It is. We just have to accept it.

I hope and will pray we all do.

It's sad to think of us saying all that Jesus did, all the mercy God gave us, wasn't enough for us to overcome and live like the royal people we are in Christ.

...But has now been revealed by the appearing of our Savior Jesus Christ, who has abolished death and brought life and immortality to light through the gospel.

2 Timothy 1:10

Chapter Eighteen

Apathy

*The hand of the LORD came upon me
and brought me out in the Spirit of
the LORD, and set me down in the midst
of the valley; and it was full of bones.
Then He caused me to pass by them all
around, and behold, there were very
many in the open valley; and
indeed they were very dry.
And He said to me, "Son of man, can
these bones live?"
So I answered, "O Lord GOD, You
know."
Again He said to me, "Prophesy to these
bones, and say to them, 'O dry bones,
hear the word of the LORD! Thus says
the Lord GOD to these bones: "Surely I
will cause breath to enter into you, and
you shall live. I will put sinews on you
and bring flesh upon you, cover you with
skin and put breath in you; and you shall*

[159]

live. Then you shall know that I am the LORD."' "

So I prophesied as I was commanded; and as I prophesied, there was a noise, and suddenly a rattling; and the bones came together, bone to bone. Indeed, as I looked, the sinews and the flesh came upon them, and the skin covered them over; but there was no breath in them.

Also He said to me, "Prophesy to the breath, prophesy, son of man, and say to the breath, 'Thus says the Lord GOD: "Come from the four winds, O breath, and breathe on these slain, that they may live."' "

So I prophesied as He commanded me, and breath came into them, and they lived, and stood upon their feet, an exceedingly great army.

Then He said to me, "Son of man, these bones are the whole house of Israel. They indeed say, 'Our bones are dry, our hope is lost, and we ourselves are cut off!' Therefore prophesy and say to them, 'Thus says the Lord GOD: "Behold, O My people, I will open your graves and cause you to come up from

*your graves, and bring you into the land of Israel. Then you shall know that I am the L*ORD*, when I have opened your graves, O My people, and brought you up from your graves. I will put My Spirit in you, and you shall live, and I will place you in your own land. Then you shall know that I, the L*ORD*, have spoken it and performed it," says the L*ORD*.'"*
Ezekiel 37:1-14

This was a vision God gave to Ezekiel when He was exiled from Jerusalem; and a very, very powerful and meaningful one. This vision is God's promise that He will restore Israel.

You see, God breathed upon the dry bones. *And they lived.*

We have some pretty dry bones, too.

Apathy is a deadly poison to us all. Apathy in the church and in Christians is too far spread.

We are supposed to be alive in Christ and bring forth His works.

Instead, we go through the motions and have no enthusiasm or interest.

This is a major disease with Christians that must be stopped.

I heard my Daddy and Grand-G saying once that people aren't hungry like they used to be. And it's true. We aren't hungry for the power of the Holy Ghost.

We need God to breathe upon *our* dry bones.

In the verse above (verse 3) God asked Ezekiel if he thought they could live. Do we think we can live again? Do we think the power of the Holy Ghost can come upon us and we rise up as the children of God we are supposed to be?

God says we can. In the verses above He put flesh and breath into completely dry, dry bones.

Do we think He can do that for us? Do we really?

He can. And it's time we got out of the danger and evil of apathy and rose up as the warriors Christ calls us to be. We need to put on the armor of God, walking forth in Jesus (Ephesians 6:10-18). We need to praise Him, being serious, and wholehearted with our lives toward Him. Declaring Him to others.

Not just living for Him for awhile, then tiring of it and letting our Spiritual life die. We need to follow the callings He as for us, and not quit when things get hard. Not quitting because we're ashamed and tired of not being popular. But rather rise up in our schools and declare His goodness. Defying drugs, alcohol, loose sex, age lies, and anything that is not of God. Saying, "YES, GOD! HERE I AM, SEND ME! I WANT TO SERVE YOU WITH MY WHOLE HEART. I WANT TO HONOR YOU! I CHOOSE TO FORSKAE APATHY AND LEAVE THE GRAVE JUST AS THE SOLDIERS DID IN EZIEKEL. I WANT TO BE AN ARMY FOR YOU! I CHOOSE TO BE!"

Let's pray by the power of the Holy Ghost for revival on our lives and on the lives of the whole world! *Pray that apathy be crushed!*

People have lost hope, like Israel in the passage above (verse 11). We've lost hope in relationships, and just peace in general. But we need to learn to hope again, God said it does not disappoint (Romans 5:5). Sure, this world seems hopeless, and there is a lot of darkness, but we are not of this world. We are of the Kingdom of Heaven!

Jesus can raise bones to life. And we need to invite Jesus to breathe on us. We need to come forth out of our graves and live.

And the devil will try and make us ashamed. He'll try and make us too shy to share Christ in our schools, work places, and homes. He's tried this all with me. And I've not mastered it at all. But God can breathe upon our shyness, and bring forth boldness.

If My people who are called by My name will humble themselves, and pray and seek My face, and turn from their wicked ways, then I will hear from heaven, and will forgive their sin and heal their land.

1 Chronicles 7:14

Chapter Nineteen

Watch and Pray

" 'And it shall come to pass in the last days, saith God, I will pour out of my Spirit upon all flesh: and your sons and your daughters shall prophesy, and your young men shall see visions, and your old men shall dream dreams: And on my servants and on my handmaidens I will pour out in those days of my Spirit; and they shall prophesy' "
Acts 2:17-18 (KJV)

This is the prophetic word God gave my Daddy when I was still a baby. It has been spoken over me my whole life.

Skip up seventeen years and I'm at a pond praying for my generation, and then my prayer goes to all generations. I'm praying that the Holy Spirit be on us, that the lies of age be defied.

Then it spreads into more than just a prayer but a vision. A vision for this message God has used me to write and be carried to the whole world. God has given me such vision. Praise HIM.

Skip back almost a week and I'm reading this passage of scripture in studies for this book, and God enlightens me. This passage is the message God has given me to take to the world. The word God has spoken over my life is the word He's given me to speak to generations in this book.

Like wow, God.

I'm so awed, overwhelmed, and excited.

God's going to perform!

Isn't God wonderful? He takes someone so incapable like me and chooses me for this. He could have chosen any number of people more qualified, I know, but He chose me! Wow!

I will pray that you carry this message away and live it. Can you believe God has taught me things right as I write them? He is God, there is none other.

Let's live like children of our Daddy. Let's start being honorable men and women and saying no more to the ways of the devil! Let's step into His light and walk in peace. Shoulders back, head up, confident in our God!

I leave you with one last message. And that's this: *There is a war waged against you.* The enemy of our soul is running rampant and he knows his time is short, so he's coming harder than ever before. *Be sober, be vigilant; because your adversary the devil walks about like a roaring lion, seeking whom he may devour,* 1 Peter 5:8. He's seeking to devour us and destroy us, and take us away from God. He's delighted when Christians are snobs. He's delighted when a teen boy takes a gun and shoots up our schools. He's delighted when someone self-harms themselves or ends their life. He's delighted when innocent people are trafficked and abused. He's delighted when someone falls away from Christ. He's delighted when we sleep around and relationships fail. He's delighted when we dwell in shame instead of accepting Christ.

And all the time these things are happening, Jesus is stretching out His nailed-scarred hands saying, *"Come to Me, all you who labor and are heavy laden, and I will give you rest..."* Matthew 11:28.

Oh, let's come.

We're living in the last days. Jesus is coming sooner or later but it will be relatively soon. And Jesus gives us a command. And that's to *watch.*

In Mark 14:38, when Jesus was fixing to be arrested and killed, He said this to His disciples, *"Watch and pray, lest you enter into temptation. The spirit indeed is willing, but the flesh is weak."*

The devil is going to try and get us...but let's watch and pray. Let's stay rooted in Christ' Word so we recognize these attacks from the enemy. Let's be friends of God...not of this world.

Jesus said watch. We don't know the exact time He's coming, but we do know the signs He's given us are happening.

He says watch. *"Watch therefore, for you do not know when the master of the house is coming—in the evening, at midnight, at the crowing of the rooster,*

*or in the morning—lest, coming
suddenly, he find you sleeping. And
what I say to you, I say to all: Watch!"*
Mark 13:35-37.

Do we want to be sleeping when He
comes? Do we want to fall for the lies of
the enemy and completely fall away
from God?

Let's say no, and rise up and...be
watchful.

The darkness in this world is great and
it may seem to outweigh any light or
hope. But God says something different.

*And the light shines in the darkness,
and the darkness did not comprehend it,*
John 1:5.

The darkness can't stand against
Jesus. It can't stand against what He's
done. And with us living out His plan,
living the honorable lives He's called us
to live, living like children of the King, I
think the landslide is going to go to
Jesus.

Now I know there will always be
darkness in this world. The devil will
always be running rampant. But in our
lives-and in the lives around us-the
darkness can vanish through Jesus

Christ! And, when the darkness tries to come again...we can, again and again, win against it.

So, are you rising up, mighty Warriors? Are you standing on the enemy and holding Jesus hand and marching toward Him.

I see you standing; everywhere, every race, and every gender.

And I hear it, too; I hear the darkness trembling-vanishing-at the sound of our Mighty Jesus!

...But one thing I do, forgetting those things which are behind and reaching forward to those things which are ahead, I press toward the goal for the prize of the upward call of God in Christ Jesus.

Philippians 3:13-14

*Therefore we also, since we are
surrounded by so great a cloud of
witnesses, let us lay aside every weight,
and the sin which so easily
ensnares us, and let us run with
endurance the race that is set before us,
looking unto Jesus, the author
and finisher of our faith, who for the joy
that was set before Him endured the
cross, despising the shame, and has sat
down at the right hand of the throne of
God. For consider Him who endured
such hostility from sinners against
Himself, lest you become weary and
discouraged in your souls*

Hebrews 12:1-3.

A word from Beth:

"For if you remain completely silent at this time, relief and deliverance will arise for the Jews from another place, but you and your father's house will perish. Yet who knows whether you have come to the kingdom for *such* a time as this?"

Esther 4:14

Wow, praise God! Almost a year later, and the second time starting this book, God has been like WOW! YEAH! AND, OH, YEAH!

The spiritual battles I've faced when I got serious about this book were ones I certainly didn't want to face, but praise God, He turned it all around for good! He freed me of things

I've been struggling with for years!
"Praise You, Jesus." And He made me
confident in His word and what I
believe! You have no idea what a
freedom this is for me! And I'm
continuing to be free.

Something else He did was teach me
as I wrote. I would write things and
He would teach me as I typed it. It's
amazing!

He gave me an amazing prayer team
and support group!

He's been the #1 Supporter in this
whole passion and calling. Hey, this is
Him. He's just using me to write.

It wasn't the passion and calling it
is now when I first started writing
this book. The spark has turned into a
flame.

I'm so grateful for my wonderful family and friends, who support and love me! And my amazing prayer team! Thank you from the bottom of my heart; you have one of the most important roles in this book!

How blessed am I that my God would choose someone as insignificant as me to do this. He. Chooses. Me. And I'm so grateful and SO blessed!

He's truly, in my own life, made the darkness tremble. Praise The Light!

With love,

Beth jane

Keep up with me on Instagram, @bethjane_author

Resources from this Book:

1: Isabella Morganthal's website:

https://isabellamorganthal.weebly.com

2: a message to my fellow collage age friends-

Sadie Robertson. Can be found on YouTube.

3: You don't have to be depressed-Savannah

Lewie. Can be found on YouTube.

4: Keith Moore message, Always Triumph, can

be found on his website, www.moorelife.org, and

on Featured Messages.

5: OBEDIENCE ‖ whole heart, whole blessing-

kirbyisaboss. Can be found on YouTube.

6: Eight Days Of Hope website,

https://eightdaysofhope.com

For you were once darkness, but now you are light in the Lord. Walk as children of light.

Ephesians 5:8

24767284R00098

Made in the USA
Columbia, SC
27 August 2018